A HIT DOG WILL HOLLER
AS IT PLEASES GOD®

DR. Y. BUR

A Hit Dog Will Holler

Copyright © 2024 by Dr. Y. Bur. All rights reserved.

Visit www.RoarPublishingGroup.com for more information. No part of this publication may be reproduced, stored in a retrieval system, or transmitted in any way by any means, electronic, mechanical, photocopy, recording, or otherwise, without the prior permission of the author except as provided by USA copyright law.

Book design copyright © 2024 by R.O.A.R. International Group. All rights reserved.

R.O.A.R. Publishing Group
581 N. Park Ave. Ste. #725
Apopka, FL 32704
www.RoarPublishingGroup.com

Published in the United States of America
ISBN: 978-1-948936-85-9
$22.88

Send *As It Pleases God* ®
Book Series **and** *Workbook* **Testimonies, Donations, Questions, or Orders to:**

Dr. Y. Bur
R.O.A.R. Publishing Group
581 N. Park Ave. Ste. #725
Apopka, FL 32704
ROAR-58-2316
762-758-2316
Dr.YBur@gmail.com

Visit Us At:
 AsItPleasesGodMovement
 AsItPleasesGod

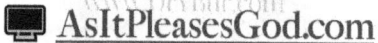 DrYBur.com
AsItPleasesGod.com

Please Donate

Please DONATE to this *Missionable Movement of God* as a GIVE-BACK to the Kingdom. Thanks for your support. Many Blessings.

AIPG Donation Link

Scan to Pay

THE THRONE ROOM

AS IT PLEASES GOD

ASITPLEASESGOD.COM

Available Titles

ASITPLEASESGOD.COM

Table of Contents

INTRODUCTION 9
CHAPTER 1 15
  ON THE DEFENSE 15
    The Vent *19*
    Humility *22*
CHAPTER 2 25
  POINT OF VIEW 25
    The Opinion *28*
    Hole In The Bucket *31*
CHAPTER 3 37
  FEAR TACTICS 37
    Anger *41*
CHAPTER 4 47
  DIY PROJECT 47
    Spiritual Tilling *50*
CHAPTER 5 53
  SELF-TALK 53
    Enthusiasm *57*
CHAPTER 6 59
  SELF-AWARENESS 59
    Obedience *64*
CHAPTER 7 69
  PEOPLE SKILLS 69

CHAPTER 8 75
A Hit Dog Will Holler 75
Respectfulness 81

CHAPTER 9 87
Overcome Distractions 87
The Antidote 89
Playing Field 92

CHAPTER 10 101
Iron Sharpens Iron 101
Faith 107

CHAPTER 11 115
Stepping Stone 115

CHAPTER 12 125
Multiplying Factors 125
Hand To Finger Approach 129
Divine Reformation 132
The Divine Plan 134
Prayer Closet 136

Introduction

Are you hit? Are you hollering? Either way, in this book, *A Hit Dog Will Holler*, our goal is to explore the complexities of human emotions and the social dynamics that we tend to overlook or sweep under the rug. When dealing with the intricate web of human relations, although no one is exempt from *The Hit Dog Hollering* charactorial traits, we must learn how to identify and deal with them, *As It Pleases God*, and not to please ourselves.

On this Spiritual Journey, through the selfless acts of regrafting or tweaking of our known and unknown habits, thoughts, desires, and propensities conveyed in this book, we can become the Crème de la Crème of Divine Greatness. Nevertheless, as this narrative unfolds, we must know what to do and how to do so, according to Kingdom Standards.

The regrafting of our character or being intellectually pristine is something most people do not understand. Nor do they realize its value. In a world where values shift with the winds of popular opinions, likes, clicks, or demands, we cannot overlook what makes *A Hit Dog Holler*.

In our self-discovering phase of life, we have a plethora of self-help books that promise quick fixes, superficial guidelines, or temporary remedies without Spiritual Healing and character development. While some advice may prove useful, it will only get us so far without God Almighty, our Heavenly Father, the Creator of it all.

Why are we limited in such a capacity, especially when information is information and we have free will to choose? First, we cannot navigate the complexities of life alone without Spiritual Guidance because we are Spiritual Beings having a human experience. Secondly, despite our choices, without having our Spiritual Governing Factors in place, *As It Pleases God*, rest assured, *A Hit Dog Will Holler*, especially when they are guilty of founded accusations, justifiable dislikes, relevant criticism, or are *On The Defense*. Thirdly, without a profound transformation, *As It Pleases God*, selfishness will continually come knocking on our doors with all types of distractions, lusts, and insinuations.

In the Kingdom, without exhibiting positive character traits, such as love, humility, compassion, and resilience, red flags are raised in the Realm of the Spirit. What is more, when we do not pursue Divine Wisdom and Understanding, *As It Pleases God*, we become loud and boastful, seeking attention with our words, desires, allurements, style of dress, or manipulative factors to portray courage and confidence. For instance, if we are the loudest person in the room, it is a silent indication that we could be the weakest link or the easiest to yoke without knowing it, while appearing strong and outgoing.

In the Eye of God, or better yet, from His *Point of View*, we are all created with a different mission as opposed to the next man, but we are all given something to work with. Nonetheless, once the *As It Pleases God* process is mastered on whatever we are working with, we can overcome and deflate the *Fear Tactics* of the *Hit Dog That Is Hollering*. In addition, we are better able to find ways to maintain a balanced lifestyle mentally, physically, emotionally, spiritually, socially, economically, and relationally.

More importantly, we must govern our tongues accordingly and remain calm as we become our own *DIY Project*. If not, in time, we will begin reacting defensively or have bouts of anger.

Just like a dog that gets hit will yelp or bark, a person who feels attacked or called out may respond similarly, causing their *Self-Talk* to become reverberated by those infected or affected, furthering the agenda. What agenda? Unfortunately, who knows the wishy-washiness of a *Hit Dog* who gets a Side-Eye from God Almighty, right? James 1:8 tells us that no one can predict a double-minded man who is unstable in all his ways.

Even if we face obstacles or challenges, a person is unpredictable when dealing with a few things, but not limited to such:

- ☐ When they are in denial of turning on themselves from the inside out.
- ☐ When seeking to please themselves at the expense of others.
- ☐ When they have nothing to lose.
- ☐ When protecting their family or livelihood.

It is often said that we do not know what we will do until we are squeezed to the max. For this reason, we must prepare ourselves to use and exhibit self-control, *As It Pleases God*.

Regardless of whether you think this book is for you or not, the Divine Principles hidden within these pages are for you and relevant to your situation. Here is what Proverbs 25:28 says about this matter: *"Whoever has no rule over his own spirit is like a city broken down, without walls."*

Our old southern proverb, *A Hit Dog Will Holler*, has come home to roost, placing my southern roots on the Doppler Radar,

As It Pleases God. All jokes aside, respectfully speaking, I am not calling anyone a dog or insulting anyone. With this book, *A Hit Dog Will Holler*, there are a few profound life-changing principles we can glean from this character trait through *Self-Awareness*.

According to the Heavenly of Heavens, we must exercise extreme caution due to the descent fermenting between the two ears of the *Hit Dog Hollering*. Whether this is within us or others, here is what Jeremiah 17:9 says about this: *"The heart is deceitful above all things, and desperately wicked; who can know it?"* Notably, most often, the one doing the hollering has something to hide or feels guilty about something. And they will fight tooth and nail to deflect what is being reflected, especially when confronted with a topic that hits too close to home or their ego is threatened. So, it behooves us to know how to deal with ourselves or someone else who is quick to respond defensively, aggressively, or dangerously. Unfortunately, this is one state of being that one must not play around with!

What do we need to do as Believers? To *Please God*, we need to take control of our consciousness and restructure our mindsets by incorporating Spiritual Laws, Principles, and Concepts. By doing so, we can enhance our *People Skills* and become better individuals in or out of the Kingdom of God. Nevertheless, if one does not like following rules or being disciplined while choosing to remain chaotic, destructive, or running scared, one must leave the restructuring process alone. We cannot run away with our tails in between our legs as if God is not who He says He is. We must come BOLDLY to the Throne of God, *As It Pleases Him*.

As a word of caution, when using Spiritual Principles for waywardness or causing harm to the innocent, it is dangerous. *"Do not be deceived: Evil company corrupts good habits."* Corinthians 15:33. The Holy Spirit will indeed convict or evict us in our wrongdoings; therefore, we must ensure that we are doing the right thing with this information.

In the *Hit Dog Will Holler* Spiritual Journey, preparing ourselves MENTALLY is the first step to the restructuring process. Regardless of who we are, why we are, or what we are going through, we must *Overcome Distractions*, preventing people from getting into our heads with negativity and debauchery.

If we allow our minds to become a cesspool, we cannot level the *Playing Field*, nor can we think on our feet, *As It Pleases God*, without tripping over our thoughts and emotions with some form of aggression. Here are the instructions from Philippians 4:7-8: *"And the peace of God, which surpasses all understanding, will guard your hearts and minds through Christ Jesus. Finally, brethren, whatever things are true, whatever things are noble, whatever things are just, whatever things are pure, whatever things are lovely, whatever things are of good report, if there is any virtue and if there is anything praiseworthy—meditate on these things."*

How do we determine the quality of our character? By our FRUITS. It is for this reason that one must also look deep down into oneself and recognize one's shortcomings or problems by owning them. Why should Believers look within first? Because *A Hit Dog* will bite, especially if they think we hate them. During this pivotal moment, if we do not put on the Whole Armor of God, we can 'get got' by the enemy's wiles.

What is the purpose of the Spiritual Armor? We must PROTECT ourselves, *As It Pleases God*, with the *Iron Sharpens Iron* mindset and the Word of God. Then we can properly enforce Psalm 91:4, saying: *"He shall cover you with His feathers, and under His wings you shall take refuge; His truth shall be your shield and buckler."*

Why must we take refuge under God's Divine Wing? A *Hit Dog That Hollers* will not sleep until they feel satisfied at seeking revenge on those who REFUSE to agree with corrupt character, bullying, or character assassination. Therefore, we must suit up, preparing ourselves with the Fruits of the Spirit and Christlike Character to deal with the wiles of a *Hit Dog*.

When approaching *As It Pleases God*, we must *Understand Our WHY*. He has zero tolerance for EXCUSES and DENIAL about corrupt character traits. Unfortunately, they can get us booted out the door or cause us to turn on ourselves. Really? Yes, really! "*He who walks with integrity walks securely, but he who perverts his ways will become known.*" Proverbs 10:9.

How do we know if we are making excuses or in denial? Lying to ourselves is a precursor to lying in the Spiritual Realm. Keep in mind that when we lie in the Spiritual Realm, it creates debauchery and deceitfulness that gives birth to the cycle of negativity, which will backfire on us in due time. If one is not ready for this Spiritual Realm of Positive Living, or if we do not plan to use it with a Positive Mental Attitude, do not tread on uncharted territory.

This book is going to give you the SECRETS on how to Regraft your character, understand when *A Hit Dog* is feeling vulnerable or defensive, and how we can best respond to them in a way that promotes open and honest communication, *As It Pleases God*.

As a TEACHER of Spiritual Truths, keep it simple, keep it positive, keep it helpful, always do what is right, exercise integrity, and exhibit a whole lot of love and peace, making it positive, productive, and fruitful, and the *Hit Dog* will stop hollering, GUARANTEED!

After reading this book, be prepared to step up into your Divine Destiny, *As It Pleases God*, or step down to prepare the way for those who have paid the price to be who they are. Either way, *The Hit Dog Will Holler* because the MANTLE is at your disposal—Use It or Lose It!

Chapter 1
On The Defense

In the Eye of God, *A Hit Dog That Hollers* is always *On The Defense*. When it comes down to dealing with a *Hit Dog*, how we deal with the issues of life will determine our level of reachability, vulnerability, pliability, and coachability. Once we learn how to manage our issues properly, we are then able to maneuver around the inevitable stresses of the wimping, venting, hollering, and complaining from the one who is always *On The Defense*.

What does dealing with ourselves have to do with handling *A Hit Dog That Hollers*? The guidelines we set for ourselves will determine whether the opinions or judgments of others easily sway us or cause us to reap by association. Plus, if we do not build ourselves up from the inside out, *As It Pleases God*, a *Hit Dog* will have us for lunch, making us their hot dogs. Why do we become meat? We are dealing with Spiritual Characteristics that will bite our heads off the moment we let our guards down.

When we are people pleasers, we will find our goals, strategies, and platforms are predicated on what people think. While receiving feedback from others can be beneficial, it is crucial to have a clear and strong sense of direction. Without clarity, we may become vulnerable to being misled, bullied, targeted, or abused. Out of all due respect, we cannot turn a deaf ear to people; however, one must know what they want and keep the influences in their life positive, productive, and fruitful, knowing when to hold, fold, or walk away.

Now, if something or someone is leading us in a different direction that is uncomfortable, contradicts our beliefs, or violates our personal space, then one must question it. I am not saying that feedback from others will always be wrong, but it may not always be right based on our experiences, perceptions, speculations, or discernment, *As It Pleases God*. The bottom line is that one must challenge or question that which may cause them to go astray, lead them in the opposite direction, or violate their conscience, especially when dealing with a *Hit Dog*.

We can go on debating all day on the various steps or approaches to how Character Development can be achieved. But, I will say this: It does not matter how much we try to remain on top of our game; we have a choice of *Pleasing God*, pleasing ourselves, or running behind a *Hit Dog* because they are hollering. What is the big deal? The Heavenly of Heavens is concerned about us, especially with what is taking place within the psyche of humanity.

What is going on with us in the Eye of God? The rise of the unshakeable longing or THIRST is upon us. It also comes with a constant reminder or alarm letting us know we need to WAKE UP to reality or make some changes before we lose our power, Spiritual Power, to be exact!

How do we make this make sense, especially when dealing with *A Hit Dog Hollering* and everyone is *On The Defense*? For example, our true POWER is in our hands...without our hands, or better yet, without our Fingerprint, we lose our identity in the real world. We often fail to recognize our uniqueness until we lose it.

Conversely, in the Spiritual World and *As It Pleases God*, we can only lose our Spiritual Power if we do not recognize it, ignore it, misuse it, do not share it *As It Pleases Him*, or forfeit it to the *Hit Dog Hollering*! Plus, the only reason they are yelping is to cause us to lose our bearings in the Eye of God.

How do we make this make sense in real life when we have real issues? If we are weak and unrepentant, the Cycle of Life begins to work against us, placing us in a cycle of déjà vu. Unfortunately, in this state, most would sell out to the highest bidder to get what they want, dealing with the lust of the eyes, the lust of the flesh, or the pride of life, which is often associated with power, money, sex, status, or fame.

Most often, it is the *Hit Dog* that will capitalize on where we are falling short, putting us in a position involving a humiliating secret or situation. At the same time, using it as leverage to keep us loyal, yoked, and fearful while inadvertently causing us to become *A Hit Puppy Hollering* to keep the cycle going. Why would we become *A Hit Puppy*? Because we have something to lose, especially if the secret is exposed. For this reason, in the Eye of God, He deals with transparency because the yoke and manipulative efforts of *A Hit Dog* are nothing to play around with.

When we set structure in our lives based upon exhibiting the Fruits of the Spirit, we are better able to weed out intruders or wolves in sheep's clothing based on their actions, character, attitude, body language, and what comes out of the gate of their mouth. Although we can sugarcoat a lot of things, when it comes down to exhibiting Godly character, it becomes challenging to do, especially if it is not in us to do so. We will slip up, and most often, it is with our tongues.

When we fake the Fruits of the Spirit, as soon as we are behind closed doors, we let it all hang out. If we pay attention long enough, people will show us who they are and what they are about. It does not matter if it is a reflection of self or a revelation of someone else...we must understand who and what we are dealing with in order to invoke, suppress, repress, oppress, or protect ourselves from the *Hit Dog Hollering*.

Listen, when we understand who we are, follow the Rules of Life, and exercise Godly Principles, we will find that all things will work out for our good. But then again, one must know this and believe it beyond a shadow of a doubt, *As It Pleases Him*.

Although no one is perfect, we are all a work-in-progress, and we are also the best version of ourselves. With this knowledge, there is no need to be on an ego trip...a super-inflated ego is an automatic indication of hidden insecurities! So, stop it!

It is the humbleness of thoughts, actions, reactions, and words that help us to keep our Spiritual Crowns, *As It Pleases God*. Who needs a Crown, right? We are all born into royalty, or we would not be here...we are here for a reason. We all have a purpose, whether we realize it or not. And the first step to owning our Crown is through gratefulness. We must learn how to appreciate and be thankful for everything: The good, the bad, and the ugly.

When we are ungrateful, it symbolically causes a downward spiral from within the depths of our souls that comes forth as envy, hatefulness, unforgiveness, ruthlessness, etc, causing us to be *On The Defense* about something or someone. We can pretend as if it is not the truth, but behind closed doors, the truth will speak whether we are listening, pouting, ignoring, sugarcoating, or just outright denying it. How? The *VENT* that we use will not lie.

The Vent

Let us discuss the importance of venting, as it is a known fact that everyone needs a way to release their frustrations, whether they realize it or not. In the Eye of God, it is essential to find healthy ways of doing so, and talking about the advantages of venting will help us understand why we must vent and what it reveals about us.

Our natural disposition enables us to express our emotions either positively or negatively through venting. Expressing our emotions through venting can be both beneficial and detrimental.

Venting can be beneficial if we have developed self-control, practical communication skills, and the ability to exhibit positive character traits like patience, kindness, goodness, gentleness, and self-control. On the other hand, if we lack these skills, venting can be detrimental and cause more harm than good, especially when becoming *A Hit Dog Hollering* and traumatizing people.

How should we vent if we are not properly equipped to vent? I would say, take a step back from the situation to think, then take out a pen and paper to ask oneself fact-finding questions to understand the *What, When, Where, How, Why,* and with *Whom* questions about the desire to vent until we cool off. What if we do not have time? It only takes a fraction of a second to oxygenate our brains; therefore, we can self-correct at the drop of a dime. Nevertheless, if we use this as an excuse, then the *Hit Dog Will Holler* analogy will apply in this case.

In my opinion, everything or everyone is not a ventable issue; it may be a soul-searching issue, it may be a lesson, it may be a blessing, etc.; so, if we pop off too soon, we will create a disservice for ourselves.

Counterproductive behavior is unacceptable as it relates to our Destined Path; we must be able to find alternative ways to redirect any deterrents that have the potential to derail us. We cannot say we are clueless about our kryptonite or triggers; we know! Although we may not admit it...deep down within the pit of our belly, we are fully aware.

According to the Heavenly of Heavens, lying to ourselves at this stage in the game will not help us; it is our transparency to the truth that lies within the depths of our soul that is going to help us deliver ourselves from ourselves.

The moment we stop lying to ourselves while getting rid of the egotistical behaviors associated with our secret envy, jealousy, coveting, and competitiveness, we are better able to contend against the enemy from within. If we do not deal with this enemy, the negativity will cause *The Hit Dog To Holler* from within us or provoke the *Hit Dogs* surrounding us.

What is the purpose of dealing with the enemy or *Hit Dog* from within ourselves? We live by example, and if that is the example we are setting for ourselves, then the gates of Hell will prevail over us. Really? Yes, really. We are designed to be a solid rock, and if we crumble under pressure in the Eye of God, we become dusted by the enemy. Please allow me to align, *As It Pleases God*: "*And I tell you, you are Peter, and on this rock, I will build my church, and the gates of hell shall not prevail against it.*" Matthew 16:18.

Who is the rock? Y.O.U. If you are oblivious to this fact, you will overlook or become unworthy of your ability to become a Spiritual Cornerstone. But if you follow my lead, "*The stone which the builders rejected will become the chief cornerstone.*" Psalm 118:22.

In my opinion, this is similar to crushing an olive to extract the oil or crushing grapes to produce wine, but in human reality. Trust me when I tell you, it will YIELD if you leave no stone unturned while opting not to throw stones or mistreat others intentionally.

Instead of throwing stones to make *A Hit Dog Holler*, we must learn how to understand and read our stones thoroughly to ensure they become Stones of Wisdom or Stepping Stones. If we are having a battle with:

- ☐ Loneliness and Neglectfulness.
- ☐ Regretfulness and Depression.
- ☐ Helplessness and Powerlessness.
- ☐ Aloofness and Aggressiveness.
- ☐ Cluelessness and Fitting In.

These are indications of overlooked Stepping Stones, or we are throwing stones containing our lessons, tests, or blessings. When we secretly or openly internalize loss, we will overlook the vital information or directions to enhance our present state, as well as our next move.

The Ancient Wisdom of yesterday has a profound impact on the way we currently live. It can also unleash secrets of universal truths, providing a Gateway to Freedom. Can we really become wise? Of course, as long as we follow the proper protocol. *"To know wisdom and instruction; to perceive the words of understanding; to receive the instruction of wisdom, justice, and judgment, and equity; to give subtilty to the simple, to the young man knowledge and discretion. A wise man will hear, and will increase learning; and a man of understanding shall attain unto wise counsels: to understand a proverb, and the interpretation; the words of the wise, and their dark sayings. The fear of the Lord is the beginning of knowledge: but fools despise wisdom and instruction."* Proverbs 1:2-7.

Humility

Most would think humility is a form of weakness; on the contrary, it is a form of hidden strength and self-control, helping us to STAY ON READY, *As It Pleases God*, without being *On The Defense*. It also helps us to develop an intimate, *Spirit to Spirit* Relationship with our Heavenly Father. Which, in my opinion, results in Supernatural Favor. When we learn how to move God, He will, in turn, move us into Divine Positioning. Furthermore, when it comes down to our lives, we have three options:

- ☐ Play by our own rules.
- ☐ Play by someone else's rules.
- ☐ Play by God's Divine Rules.

Either way, with or without a mask, we choose. For the most part, our Spiritual Classroom or Training may require us to do all three with limits and boundaries; however, playing by God's rules is Supreme and has moral and ethical standards that are enforceable, *As It Pleases Him*.

What does enforceability have to do with anything? According to the Heavenly of Heavens, once we align with Spiritual Laws, *As It Pleases God*, we can enforce them based on our Heaven on Earth Experiences. For example, "*No weapon formed against you shall prosper, and every tongue which rises against you in judgment You shall condemn. This is the heritage of the servants of the Lord, and their righteousness is from Me, Says the Lord.*" Isaiah 54:17. Most often, we use the first part of this scripture, but we do not often include the Spiritual Contingency Clause that follows, which contains the HERITAGE and RIGHTEOUSNESS part. If we hate God, ignore Him, behave waywardly without repentance, or cast wicked plots, we cannot ENFORCE this in the Name of Jesus. Why not? It is being MISUSED selfishly by forming weapons against others.

In navigating both sides of Spiritual Duality, we form fascinating, debauched, or unjustified weapons against others for self-pleasure. Yet, we do not want justified or unjustified weapons formed against us. Come on...We have to do better than this. Our weapons are SEEDS...So, we should make sure that the weapons used in living real life or in Spiritual Warfare are Godly, justified, and righteous.

God clearly unmasks, telling us throughout scripture how to PLEASE Him. He also clearly tells us what will happen if we please ourselves or hurt others in the commission of our selfishness. Just remember, it is about WILLINGNESS and OBEDIENCE when we are playing by any form of rules on any level or any playing field.

Do we think for a minute that God cannot see straight through our debaucherous masks? Of course, He can. So, who are we fooling? Ourselves, perhaps? I am not here to point any fingers; I know about masks all too well. Besides, it takes a mask to recognize one, right? I was clueless back then, but now that I know the difference, I do not wish it on anyone; therefore, I am not here to sugarcoat anything. My Spiritual Training was fierce, and I am here to bring about a radical change from within the depths of our souls, *As It Pleases God*. In doing so, here are a few things we need to know, but not limited to such:

- ☐ We need to get rid of a destructive or harmful attitude.
- ☐ We need to listen effectively without assuming.
- ☐ We need to manage our time wisely and plan effectively.
- ☐ We need to exhibit Godly values in what we do, say, and become while controlling our emotions and reactions.

- ☐ We need to focus on the objective, not the obstacle, while remaining calm, especially when provoked.
- ☐ We must be able to counteract the negatives with positive affirmations while eliminating excuses.
- ☐ We must humbly become a straight-shooter when it comes down to our integrity.
- ☐ We must avoid trying to change others; we can only change ourselves.
- ☐ We must limit our distractions.
- ☐ We must become an expert in prioritizing.
- ☐ We need to declutter our environment, as well as our minds.
- ☐ We need to reserve the right to Plead the 5th at any given moment. Why? Some things do not deserve a response.

As we unmask ourselves, we must become comfortable with being who God has designed us to be. Now, in order to do so, we must love God, we must love ourselves with our flaws and all, and we must love others, in that order. This approach helps us to become comfortable in making eye contact, finding common similarities without having a fear of not being good enough, extracting positive attributes without having to focus on the negative, building magnetic rapport, expressing how we feel without offending, helping others without expecting anything in return, and maintaining a Positive Mental Attitude.

Can this really work with *A Hit Dog Hollering*? Absolutely. However, we may have to approach from their point of view strategically. Still, with the Fruits of the Spirit, Christlike Character, the presence of the Holy Spirit, and the covering of the Blood of Jesus, it calms the human psyche naturally.

Chapter 2
Point of View

When a point of view remains unheard or ignored, it can cause a person to react strongly and make a scene, even if they do not have the opportunity to express their thoughts. This behavior can be especially noticeable in people who struggle to control their emotions, words, or thoughts. Sadly, an unheard or ignored *Point of View* will cause *A Hit Dog To Holler* to make everyone pay attention to their temper tantrum.

Our level of preparedness is what matters, not the inevitability of life. Whether we choose to play it safe with or without God, we may end up constraining our abilities and potential. In this chapter, *Point of View*, I will share information on how to capitalize on your encounters with the hollering of *A Hit Dog*.

Despite the apparent simplicity of learning, goal-setting, strategizing, developing plans, journaling, sharing, and relaxing, many of us struggle to put these practices into action while pretending to be astute at them. Although we know what to do, implementing them seems to pose a challenge. The reason for this is that we often get sidetracked from our own lives by paying too much attention to other people's lives. And when the *Hit Dog Hollers*, it ruffles our feathers because we are not prepared and have failed to work on ourselves as we should.

Many of us spend our lives striving to impress others, but the truth is that we only need to prove ourselves to ourselves, *As It Pleases God*. If we live our lives with a clear sense of purpose, we should be confident in our abilities and not feel the need to constantly prove ourselves to those who do not understand our goals and aspirations. In my opinion, living with conviction and purpose is the key to self-assurance and a fulfilling life.

If we live our lives WITHOUT a clear sense of direction, we might end up relying too much on the opinions of others. Unfortunately, this can lead us down a path of negativity that can be difficult to overcome. In the Eye of God, it is crucial to stay grounded in our beliefs and values, *As It Pleases Him*.

As we move into the things of the Spirit, when mastering our *Point of View*, it is not about who is the smartest. It is about who is the most effective, who is most purposeful, who is using their inner-born talents or giftings, who is helping, who is mentoring, who is nurturing others, and who is maximizing the Fruits of the Spirit.

When we redirect our focus to PURPOSE, we will find we have less time trying to please others and more time to provide a service or solve problems. Listen, servant leadership has more power than we care to imagine, but for some odd reason, it is overlooked because we are focused on having others serve us.

Many individuals attempt to lead selfishly through power, influence, control, and arrogance. While it may work temporarily for some, from my SPIRITUAL neck of the woods, this type of behavior is greatly frowned upon. Why is this frowned upon? We should lead, *As It Pleases God*. Not to please ourselves with God nowhere in our equational efforts.

From my *Point of View*, I am going to let you in on a little SECRET. Okay, it is a BIG SECRET...When you lead with humility, servanthood, self-control, diligence, love, and wisdom, you will find that you not only become effective, but you can also mentor on a level that will create a Legacy of Impact.

For example, think about an ant...it is diligent, it is useful, it works hard, and it does not care about what you think of it. Its goal is to serve its QUEEN by any means necessary. You will never hear an ant crying, complaining, or gossiping...they have a goal in mind, and they do not take 'NO' for an answer; they will always find a way to mastermind their ventures, surviving any form of extinction from the Ancient of Days until now!

Although our beliefs and assumptions about the underlying reasons for our life issues may hold some validity, it is crucial to engage in a more profound exploration of our psyche, *As It Pleases God*. As individuals, we must allocate adequate time to examine ourselves according to Kingdom Standards to give us a comprehensive understanding of ourselves in the Eye of God and not of man. This introspection can help us identify patterns that may be hindering our walk with Him, personal growth, and Spiritual Development.

Why should we examine ourselves from God's *Point of View*? If we cannot see ourselves first, it is a great possibility that we see others incorrectly based on our thwarted perception or state of denial. Do not worry too much about this form of Spiritual Blindness for now; it happens to all of us from time to time. I am not exempt from this...I check myself constantly in order to share information that is truthful, just, informative, inspirational, and accurate based on my experiences in life, the nudging of the Spirit, and the Fruits of the Spirit.

In the Eye of God, we are all unique with our own set of gifts, talents, knowledge, and skills. If we second-guess or doubt this fact, insecurities will come in to kill, steal, and destroy our faith and hope, allowing the *Hit Dog To Holler*, making us Spiritual Deaf and Dumb in the Realm of the Spirit. Therefore, I am going to empower you with the wisdom needed to take your life back while unraveling every knot you have created and untwisting every coil you knowingly, unknowingly, or fearfully twisted.

The Opinion

One of the most significant obstacles to achieving our desired outcomes is the impact of *Opinions*, both our own and those of others. Unfortunately, this is a crucial factor that cannot be overlooked and has an enormous influence on our journey towards success. We must recognize and address this obstacle in order to attain our goals, *As It Pleases God*.

The *Opinionated* factors associated with us must be sorted out at some point in our lives. Preferably sooner than later, but it is my reasonable service to equip everyone with the information needed to overcome, circumvent, endure, and abound. For the sake of *A Hit Dog Will Holler*, we will be dealing with five types of opinions:

- ☐ A Qualified Opinion.
- ☐ A Non-Qualified Opinion.
- ☐ An Understood Opinion.
- ☐ A Foolery Opinion.
- ☐ A Disclaimed Opinion.

The Power of Positive Expression is a blessing in itself. In my opinion, it is a compelling form of liberation that goes unrecognized or underutilized by those who need it the most. Therefore, I am going to explain how to make what does or does not come out of our mouths powerful, effective, and fruitful, *As It Pleases God.*

To begin, let us go to the Word of God for a moment. "*The entrance of Your words gives light; it gives understanding to the simple.*" Psalm 119:130. In addition, regardless of whether you are speaking in general or expressing an opinion, "*Let your speech always be gracious, seasoned with salt, so that you may know how you ought to answer each person.*" Colossians 4:6. Now, before we move on, let me break down how I define *Opinions* as they relate to mastering a *Point of View*.

- ☐ A **Qualified Opinion** or Professional Opinion gives us the right to make an opinionated statement based on our credentials, experiences, degrees, or lineages. Keep in mind that a qualified opinion does not make the statement right, wrong, or factual; it simply means we are qualified to say what we have been taught.

- ☐ A **Non-Qualified Opinion** or Non-Professional Opinion gives us the ability to make an opinionated statement without having the credentials to back it up. This does not make the statement right, wrong, or factual because it very well may be; it means we do not have the formal education, experience, degree, or lineage to give us the entitlement to have a qualified opinion.

- ☐ An **Understood Opinion** enables us to comprehend the logic behind our spoken words and even the reasoning behind our unspoken thoughts. This is the type of opinion that predicates itself on knowing and understanding the *What, When, Where, How, Why,* and the with *Whom* questions. Most often, it is used in the psychoanalysis phase when directing a question at oneself and others. But more importantly, this type of opinion gives us the ability to understand the soulish reasonings or the Spiritual Importance of exhibiting self-control, as well as the importance of NOT losing it. For *"Whoever restrains his words has knowledge, and he who has a cool spirit is a man of understanding."* Proverbs 17:27.

- A **Foolery Opinion** gives us the ability to say whatever we want or feel about anything, with or without recourse. Most often, a foolery opinion is exhibited in those who say anything they want and then try to play cleanup later. *"A fool takes no pleasure in understanding, but only in expressing his opinion."* Proverbs 18:2. Just so we are clear, I am not calling anyone a fool; I am only referring to unwise behavior. Just remember, *"Death and life are in the power of the tongue, and those who love it will eat its fruit."* Proverbs 18:21.

- A **Disclaimed Opinion** gives us the right to Plead the 5th at any given moment. The right to say nothing is the opinion of the person exhibiting their right to do so. *"Whoever keeps his mouth and his tongue keeps himself out of trouble."* Proverbs 21:23. In addition, it is also the ability to protect ourselves from the liability of people taking things the wrong way when voicing our opinions in a public or business environment. For example, when people are spreading gossip or rumors, they will preface what they are saying with 'Allegedly.' Now, from a Spiritual Perspective, this also gives us the right to interject, seal, or close our petitions to God by 'Pleading the Blood of Jesus,' or by saying, 'In the Name of Jesus' without any form of liability.

As children of God, it is important to realize that self-control is not about suppressing our thoughts, emotions, and feelings. Instead, it is the ability to comprehend our experiences, thoughts, and feelings, the reasons behind them, when they occur, where they take place, how they affect us, and with whom.

At first, it may take a little more time to psychoanalyze ourselves; yet, in the long run, once we become accustomed to asking fact-finding questions, it will become second nature, and it will only take seconds to do.

While many may overlook the importance of understanding the reasons behind their actions and decisions, I firmly believe that it is crucial for our mental well-being. Ignoring our thoughts, emotions, and feelings is not a sustainable solution, as they will inevitably continue to resurface until we identify their root cause. So, let us take charge of our lives and confidently explore the underlying reasons for our whys to attain a more fulfilling existence. Proverbs 2:2-5 says, "*Make your ear attentive to wisdom and incline your heart to understanding; yes, if you call out for insight and raise your voice for understanding, if you seek it like silver and search for it as you would for hidden treasures, then you will understand the fear of the Lord and find the knowledge of God.*"

Hole In The Bucket

The *Hole in the Bucket* analogy has caused many of us to become secretly self-righteous in our way of thinking, behaving, and judging. This specific type of grouping has caused many to overlook the eminent fact that we all have a hole within the depths of our souls. Blasphemy, right? Wrong. Holiness is all about dealing with the hole within us, not to make us better than anyone, as most would think. Psalm 42:1-2 says, *"As the deer pants for the water brooks, So pants my soul for You, O God. My soul thirsts for God, for the living God. When shall I come and appear before God?"*

Our souls cannot thrive without God, and if we think we can, we are sadly mistaken. Our well-being is dependent on our connection with the Holy Trinity, as without it, the soul cannot flourish or reach its full potential, even if we think we have it going on. Why? Our DNA is prewired with this longing connecting us from the earthly realm to the Heavenly Realm. For this reason, there is no one-size-fits-all approach to Spirituality.

All of our Predestined Blueprints are different; thus, we must develop a *Spirit to Spirit* Relationship, *As It Pleases God*, to obtain the details in totality. Although the evidence and instructions are written all over the Bible, for some reason, we ignore them to embrace the *Hole in the Bucket* mentality or become a *Hit Dog Hollering*.

What is the *Hole in the Bucket* mentality? It is a phrase used to describe a problem-solving approach where the focus is on fixing the symptoms of a problem rather than addressing the root cause. It is like trying to patch up a hole in a bucket without realizing that the real issue is the poor quality of the material used to make the bucket.

Realistically, this type of thinking can lead to a cycle of temporary fixes and quick solutions without adding God into our equational efforts. To add insult to injury, it ultimately fails to solve the problem in the long term, similar to having a leaky faucet without addressing the underlying plumbing issues, eventually causing structural water damage and mold.

According to the Heavenly of Heavens, it is crucial to IDENTIFY and ADDRESS the root cause of a problem to achieve a sustainable solution. How do we make this make sense in real life? For example, Rhonda had always been a woman of faith who wanted to be a positive role model for others and to please God. She believed that by living a virtuous life and helping those in need, she could make a difference in this world. One day, Rhonda decided that she wanted to start volunteering at a local shelter for people without housing. She felt that this was a calling from God and was excited to begin making a difference in the lives of those who were less fortunate than herself.

However, as Rhonda began to volunteer at the shelter, she noticed that many problems needed to be addressed. The shelter was overcrowded, the facilities were inadequate, they did not have enough beds, they had a shortage of blankets, the roof was leaking, and the staff was overworked and underpaid. Despite these issues, Rhonda continued to volunteer at the shelter, believing that she was doing the right thing by helping those in need.

However, as time went on, Rhonda began to realize that her efforts were not having the impact that she had hoped for. As a result, she began to feel discouraged, wondering if her efforts were in vain as she watched innocent people suffer from lack. As Rhonda left the shelter with a heavy heart, it was only then that she realized that she had fallen into the *Hole in the Bucket* mentality. Instead of addressing the underlying issues, she continued to volunteer at a shelter that was not equipped to handle the needs of the displaced community.

Rhonda realized that if she genuinely wanted to make a difference, she needed to address the underlying issues and work towards creating a better system for the shelter. She began to research different ways to support the shelter, such as fundraising initiatives and spreading awareness about the needs of people without housing.

By addressing these underlying issues, Rhonda was able to make a much more significant impact than she could have ever had by simply continuing to volunteer at the shelter. She became a positive role model for others in her community, inspiring them to take action and make a difference in the lives of those who were less fortunate.

In the end, Rhonda learned that by addressing the underlying issues and working towards creating lasting change, she could truly please God and make a positive impact on the world.

The moment we get beside ourselves to point the finger at someone else's hole without offering them a Godly solution, our hole becomes bigger as a result. Our very own psychological trauma becomes more intense, our fears become overbearing, our trust is out the window, and the list goes on. However, we have the POWER to fill the hole by pinpointing the leak.

In my opinion, the HOLE is basically a VOID. And the only reason *A Hit Dog Will Holler* is due to this hole. Suppose we reverse the word void to diov. This is what it means to me: DI = Die and OV = Of. Although this is hidden in plain sight, we often miss what a void will do to us, Mentally, Physically, Emotionally, and Spiritually. To **DIE OF** something that we have no clue about or how we are contributing to our own detriment is an atrocity in the Eye of God.

I am not here to play on words; I am here to open our Spiritual Eyes to what is really happening within the depths of our souls in spite of the *Hole in the Bucket's* superficial reasoning. I do not want anyone to die of any form of void or hole in their Mind, Body, Soul, or Spirit, so I am sharing this information because the yelp of the *Hit Dog* is vibrating to the FOUR CORNERS of the earth.

Will we ever get rid of our void? The answer is 'no;' it is intertwined in our DNA because we are Spiritual Beings having a human experience. Therefore, it is somewhat controlled, keeping us dependent upon God, and ensuring we do not place ourselves above Him! Even if we try, we will fail at our attempts because the psyche of man is subservient to the Spirit. Blasphemy, right? Wrong.

The moment we consciously or unconsciously renounce our need for God, we become self-righteous, and our insecurities will bubble over into our thoughts, actions, reactions, and conversations. According to scripture, here is what it says about self-righteousness: *"For they being ignorant of God's righteousness, and going about to establish their own righteousness, have not submitted themselves unto the righteousness of God."* Romans 10:3.

God can and will heal us from the Mental, Physical, Emotional, or Spiritual effects of a void to prevent triggers, or He will help us uproot the negative character traits associated with the non-conducive residues. In my opinion, this is similar to having a topical sore on our skin; once the sore heals, the scar may not be seen with the naked eye, but under a microscope or with a thorough examination, it can be seen.

According to the Heavenly of Heavens, small changes can lead to big results if we place God first, *As It Pleases Him*. So, we must escape the *Hole in the Bucket* mindset to ensure the *Hit Dog Will Not Holler* when we least expect it. How? Here is a list to help, but not limited to such:

- ☐ Pinpoint the root of the issue and fix it with problem-solving techniques.
- ☐ Focus on solutions instead of problems.
- ☐ Take action.
- ☐ Identify and replace negative self-talk.

- ☐ Use positive affirmations.
- ☐ Focus on the good and give thanks for all things.
- ☐ Develop a growth mindset.
- ☐ Focus on learning and improving.
- ☐ Set achievable goals and make a plan to reach them.
- ☐ Learn to recognize triggers.
- ☐ Manage negative emotions like fear, insecurity, and self-doubt.
- ☐ Identify your strengths.
- ☐ Understand your weaknesses.
- ☐ Forgive and repent often.
- ☐ Shift your perspective from scarcity to abundance.

The *Hole in the Bucket* mentality should not limit us. Pictorially, if we create mind maps, develop systems, or a schedule for ourselves, we are better able to stay on track while developing ourselves to become better, stronger, and wiser, *As It Pleases God*, without giving way to *Fear Tactics*.

www.DrYBur.com

Chapter 3
Fear Tactics

The expression, '*A Hit Dog Will Holler*,' is a fear-inducing strategy or *Fear Tactic* used to silence someone who calls out a person on their behavior or actions. The idea is that if someone reacts defensively or aggressively to a criticism or accusation, it is a sign that they feel personally attacked and may have something to hide. By understanding this tactic, we can better navigate difficult conversations and stand up for ourselves without succumbing to the fear and intimidation that often accompany it.

It is imperative to comprehend the significance of understanding the underlying causes of our fears, as they can take on various forms and play a crucial role in our overall development. By identifying the root cause of our fears, we gain important insights into how they manifest in our lives and how they may be overcome. This knowledge can help us to better address and manage our fears, both in personal and professional contexts. Ultimately, a deep understanding of our fears can lead to improved decision-making, increased self-awareness, and greater overall success in our endeavors.

As life would have it, when building a house into a home, we must understand the difference between our level of fear, as well as our ability to choose between good and evil, right and wrong, positive and negative, etc. On behalf of this book, I am going to share the good, right, and positive side of your Character Traits and how to make them work in your favor.

We all have several fears: The fear of getting hurt, the fear of being cheated on, the fear of dying, the fear of separation, the fear of rejection, the fear of losing our jobs, the fear of not being able to pay our bills, and the list goes on! Many of our fears are not real; they are ROOTED in delusional impulses, confusing our perception in a way that causes our fears to appear real.

How we perceive ourselves and the people, places, and things around us determines our reality, but it does not make our reality real or factual; it merely determines how we see it. If we learn how to take control of our attitude and relax, *As It Pleases God*, we will find that all things will work together for our good as long as we do not fear it or taint our perception of it.

Fear is not necessarily a negative emotion as long as we handle it correctly, *As It Pleases God*. In fact, a balanced amount of fear can be beneficial for us, provided that we comprehend it. It can alert us to genuine dangers and help us avoid them. However, we should only rely on fear as a temporary measure until we address the root causes of our insecurities and vulnerabilities through Spiritual Growth, inner peace, and mindset strengthening. Once we achieve this goal, we can become Spiritually Fearless, possessing an unshakable confidence that transcends human understanding.

If we wallow in our fears and embrace our ability to remain afraid of things we cannot control, then it becomes an unhealthy fear and not a survival mechanism. If we allow fear to become our shadow, we will become susceptible to becoming overbearing and controlling. Then again, we can become weak, easily influenced, or bullied.

Fear crushes our self-reliance, enthusiasm, and initiative, promoting procrastination and leading to weak character. In addition, fear defeats our ability to love efficiently and effectively, *As It Pleases God*. Without love, our fears will eventually lead to known or unknown misery, heartaches, betrayal, and sadness. However, we must not lose hope, as fear and a lack of courage are simply states of mind that can be overcome by reshaping our character and embracing our unique traits.

Our faith is our power! Without it, life becomes a little more complicated to understand, which causes us to fear and judge life through our own eyes, with our perception of God nowhere in our equational efforts. When it comes down to the root of our fears, our perception must meet up with the truth of our reality.

Of course, no one gloats over misbehaving unless they are trying to fit in or prove something to someone or control them. Believe it or not, behind closed doors, the conscience does take over, especially in the wee hours of the night. Most often, this is the reason why some cannot sleep at night, this is the reason why nightmares paralyze us, and this is the reason why we become addicted. What is the purpose of this happening to us? The reasons may vary; however, the conscience is not something we should ignore because the psyche will do a number on us to the point where we do not know if we are coming or going.

As we look for external occurrences of the Wrath of God, they take place within the psyche as internal manifestations, making the *Hit Dog Holler* loud, exuding deafening sounds of disgruntlement. Please allow me to Spiritually Align before going any further. *"For the people do not turn to Him who strikes them, Nor do they seek the LORD of hosts. Therefore the LORD will cut off head and tail from Israel, Palm branch and bulrush in one day. The elder and honorable, he is the head; The prophet who teaches lies, he is the tail. For the leaders of this people cause them to err, And those who are led by them are destroyed. Therefore the Lord will have no joy in their young men, Nor have mercy on their fatherless and widows; For everyone is a hypocrite and an evildoer, And every mouth speaks folly. For all this His anger is not turned away, But His hand is stretched out still."* Isaiah 9:13-17.

We can sugarcoat the conscience as much as we like! Still, it does not mean the Eye of God is not watching and monitoring us closely. My goal is to get to the root of the *Fear Tactics*, which are keeping you up at night, whatever is chasing you in your dreams, whatever is causing you to become numb, whatever is keeping you addicted, and whatever is sucking the life out of you.

According to the social statistics, we pride ourselves on becoming virally famous at all costs...where have we gone so wrong? I am so glad you asked! What God has for you is for you...You do not have to sell your soul to get it! You do not have to fuss or fight to get it. You do not have to pimp or prostitute to get it. You do not have to throw people under the bus to get it! Your goodness has enough power to get you whatever you need, and you do not have to bow down to the *Hit Dog Hollering*. If you do not have it, exhibit PATIENCE as you follow my lead in this book. After doing so, if it is for you, it will come. If not, then it was not good for you and not a part of your Divine Blueprint. In my opinion, that is a BLESSING in itself.

So, the Spirit of Anger should never become our portion. What does this mean in layman's terms? Fear and anger go hand in hand, like twin siblings containing their own identities. With God, we can separate the two, *As It Pleases Him*. On the other hand, without Him, they will never leave the other one behind. Nonetheless, let us get in the know about the *Fear Tactics* associated with *Anger*.

Anger

Anger is a common emotion; it is also one of the most mismanaged emotions known to man. The Bible says, *"Be ye angry, and sin not: let not the sun go down upon your wrath."* Ephesians 4:26. The reason we cannot allow the sun to go down on our anger is the fact that harboring anger has Spiritual Implications that manifest into other negative attributes as we sleep. When we have anger inside of us that is simmering all night long, by the time we wake up, our anger is boiling over! The goal is not to allow our anger to consume us; if it does, it leads to other negative emotions such as hatefulness, unforgiveness, unkindness, rudeness, revenge, etc.

Our quality of life is paramount; we should not subject ourselves to the Spirit of Anger when we have the power to cast it down. I have found that some people who are dealing with anger issues do not realize they truly have power over it, and they can cast it out on their own, self-correcting themselves. Instead, they allow it to manifest and grow out of control, creating a dense layer of sludge over the psyche. Although sometimes it may be a Spiritual Issue, we still have power over it if we believe we do, especially when using a Spiritual Mirror, *As It Pleases God*.

Our negative self-talk contributes to and fuels our anger. How is it possible to fuel anger, especially as Believers, knowing and speaking the Word of God over our lives? I cannot determine what measures of Spiritual Means we use to fuel or deflate our inner chatter or anger as Believers; God must determine this and its worthiness. However, I can speak about the unfailing truths of our DNA, or better yet, our human nature. Whether we are pro-positive or pro-negative, Pro-God or Anti-God, we all have triggers, and no one is exempt from fear or anger. Why? God has designed them to save our lives when faced with danger; however, we must learn how to use them, *As It Pleases Him*. Not to please ourselves, selfishly misuse them, or bring harm to another without just cause.

Our minds can rehearse an issue over and over again, creating all types of illusions and scenarios, even if we pretend it cannot. And, until we put a stop to it, our minds will continue adding issues that may not have any form of truth or relevancy, asking questions that create paranoia, and planting seeds of worry that will not solve problems but create them instead.

When our minds are clouded with negative self-talk, it blocks out our positive rationalization skills. The best way to bring a halt to harmful behavior is to cancel or rebuke it, counteract the negative with a positive, and find the scripture that applies to the situation, emotion, thought, action, or reaction.

Can we really control our anger? The answer is 'Yes.' When we feel the sense of anger coming, we must cut it off, cancel it, or rebuke it. How is this possible, right? Here is what I do: I stop what I am doing; if I cannot stop...I am slow to respond, thinking through every word or thought, and I will smile or giggle to get into my happy space. Then, once I am done, I walk away, take a deep breath, and I visually push away the anger when breathing out. Once we make the conscious choice to be at peace and remain calm, we are better able to manage our anger. James 1:19 tells us, *"Everyone must be quick to hear, slow to speak and slow to anger."*

How can we become slow to speak when fear and anger are in our faces with their horns reared? For example, the moment

I am feeling fearful, here is what I would say audibly or inaudibly: I cancel out the Spirit of Fear; I send it back into the Pits of Hell from whence it came. In the Name of Jesus, I usher in the Spirit of Courage, *"For God has not given me a spirit of fear, but of power and of love and of a sound mind."* 2 Timothy 1:7. It is for this that I give thanks. Amen.

The moment I feel anger rising from within, here is what I say: I rebuke the Spirit of Anger; I send it back into the Pits of Hell from whence it came. In the Name of Jesus, I usher in the Spirit of Peace. Father, You said: *"You will keep me in perfect peace if my mind is stayed on You, as long as I put my trust in You."* Isaiah 26:3. Therefore, *"I am casting all my anxieties on You."* It is for this that I give thanks. Amen.

When canceling, replacing, and sealing the covenant with God through scriptures, it is okay to personalize them to fit our conversations with God. However, when canceling a negative trait or attribute, we cannot just cancel it without replacing it. If we cancel without replacing it, then what is going to take the place of what we canceled? My point exactly! NOTHING! If we do not fill in the blank, we leave this blank open for another negative trait or attribute to take its place, and it defeats the purpose. Therefore, we must complete the process...when we remove or cancel, we must replace it with something positive with scripture to back it up. Spiritually, this is crucial; we do not want to leave ourselves open to an attack from the enemy. Here is the sample format, but not limited to such:

I cancel out the Spirit of _____; *I send it back into the Pits of Hell from whence it came. In the Name of Jesus, I usher in the Spirit of*_____, SCRIPTURE "_____."

If we are still frustrated, we can take a walk, pray, dance, or workout to release the bottled-up energy. Never become accusatory or point the finger...it depletes our power. When expressing how we feel, speak in the "I" form, not the "You" form. For example: You did this, you did that...the you, you, you, is out! Here is what I would say, "I allowed myself to get upset because of _____." "I got a little frustrated because _____." "I apologize for getting upset because I felt that _____." When we own how we feel, we are able to take action and shift the atmosphere or energy. However, if we deny it, then there is nothing to resolve. I would say go ahead, own it, and get over it quickly.

Why must we go through all of this regarding anger? Our anger is two-fold. It can work for us as a means of motivation, or it can be used as a tool to destroy us, as well as others. The signs of anger problems from others can also give us a warning about things to come. When people show us who they are, we must believe them to safeguard our sanity.

According to Proverbs 22:24, it says, *"Do not associate with a man given to anger, or go with a hot-tempered man."* Plus, if we try to put up a smoke screen regarding our anger, it will cause us to become Mentally, Emotionally, Physically, and Spiritually tapped out, causing temper tantrums when we least expect them. It takes a lot of energy to become angry, stay angry, and hold a grudge. Besides, we can only hide our anger for a certain amount of time before the mask comes off.

Aggression, violence, and disrespectfulness are the result of undealt with, untreated, or unresolved anger and fear. In today's time, some people think it is cool or funny to pop off, but in all actuality, our anger can create a great disservice.

Broken homes, broken relationships, broken hearts, broken anything may be a result of anger in some way, shape, or form. We need to know what triggers our anger and the reasons why.

We must get to the root. What if there is no root? In the Eye of God, if there is anger, there is a ROOT. It is our responsibility to find what irritates us, what provokes us, or what causes displeasure.

Fighting, screaming, fussing, and mistreating others like *A Hit Dog Hollering* are not conducive to deflating anger; actually, they are fuel. They ignite anger in ways that are beyond our human comprehension. *"Do not be eager in your heart to be angry, for anger resides in the bosom of fools."* Ecclesiastes 7:9.

Road rage is a prime example of uncontrollable anger and foolishness when, in all actuality, driving is a privilege as well as a blessing. How can someone overlook this fact? We forget to count our small blessings...allowing a miniscule emotion such as anger to have control over us. Having a short fuse is no excuse for exhibiting bad behavior or a bad attitude...we are required to make the appropriate adjustments in the Root of our Character. According to James 1:20, *"Anger of man does not achieve the righteousness of God."*

"A hot-tempered man stirs up strife, but the slow to anger calms a dispute." Proverbs 15:18. There are times we may have to distance ourselves from the people, places, and things that provoke us to anger so we can embrace the elements of calmness or patience.

We are not required to respond to our anger or the anger of someone else. *"A man's discretion makes him slow to anger, and it is his glory to overlook a transgression."* Proverbs 19:11. When we value our peace, we are not so quick to give it up. We are quick to forgive or ask for forgiveness. We are quick to apologize. We are quick to say, 'Thank You!' And, we are quick to respond in a kind tone of voice because *"A gentle answer turns away wrath, but a harsh word stirs up anger."* Proverbs 15:1.

Remember, we have the authority and the power to cast down or cast out any and all negative attributes. We do not have to depend upon anyone to do it for us—we simply need the right Spiritual Tools and use the proper Spiritual Protocol when doing so.

Do not forget that the Word of God is our Spiritual Ammunition. From this point on, it is time out for the *Woe Unto Me* mentality because we are our best *DIY Project* known to man. We have everything we need inside of us.

Chapter 4
DIY Project

Embarking on a *DIY Project* with ourselves, *As It Pleases God*, can be a fun, rewarding, and fulfilling experience. Unleashing our creativity and imagination unselfishly on ourselves is not often a project we engage in as Believers or *As It Pleases Him*. The ability to create something out of nothing or what is already is a GIFT that we should all cherish and cultivate. According to the Heavenly of Heavens, no one is exempt from the DIY abilities unless we become *A Hit Dog Hollering*, cause mass destruction in the psyche of weaker vessels, or intentionally spread false narratives.

And, as it turns out from the Ancient of Days, becoming our best DIY project is a great way to make weaker vessels stronger and stronger vessels POWERFUL. Really? Yes, really! In the Eye of God, our Spiritual strength is hidden in peace and calmness. Taking the time and effort to improve ourselves, *As It Pleases God*, comes with fringe benefits, which happen to be peace and calmness. Most often, we search for them in people, places, and things, but it is time to look from within.

In today's day and age, everyone is busy doing something, but very few people have the energy to take their lives to the next level to bring about the precious commodity of calmness. Still, we prefer success to be packaged in a box or microwavable, not realizing that true and lasting success is indeed a DIY project.

How can peace and calmness be a DIY Project? We must recognize our weaknesses, work to overcome them, Spiritually Till our own ground, and strive to become the best version of ourselves, doing all things in the Spirit of Excellence, *As It Pleases God*. How is it going to grant calmness to the ones who need it? No one can do calm for us...The true awakening of our CALM requires us to develop our peacefulness, patience, perseverance, concentration, and self-development constantly due to the many distractions surrounding us.

What type of distractions are we faced with? I am so glad you asked! Our modern conveniences include electronic equipment, gadgets, cell phones, and tools, as well as entertainment through television, magazines, and social media. With the abundance of things...we become distracted with our physical needs and wants. As a result, our concepts of self-worth and self-meaning are topsy-turvy.

Whether we are learning a new skill, understanding our Divine Purpose, overcoming a bad habit, or just trying to be a better person, we should always strive to do so in a way that honors God, brings glory to His name, and sheds LIGHT on the Kingdom, *As It Pleases Him*. Why? In the Eye of God, it may provide the medicine to our NEXT whatever, whomever, or whyever. Proverbs 20:30 says, *"The scars of past wounds are medicine for evil and living reproof reaches the most secret places in the inward parts."*

How can we find a balance between the Material, Emotional, Mental, Physical, and Spiritual aspects of our lives while being surrounded by this social explosion? We must query ourselves by asking, 'Are we *Pleasing God*, ourselves, or someone else?' To regraft our lives, we must look inward while resisting the temptation to get caught up in wasting time on people, places, and things that are not building us or taking us to the next level of living, *As It Pleases Him*.

Self-examination goes beyond recalling the things that happened to us...We must look closely at the reflection of our thoughts, actions, reactions, feelings, attitudes, beliefs, motives, experiences, and motivations. Now, what I have found is that when we begin to understand and master the Fruits of the Spirit, it will give us clues on how to act, react, and conduct ourselves in any situation, with the cheatsheet on how to self-correct at the drop of a dime.

Like any skill, self-examination can be learned. All it takes is the courage and willingness to seek the truth that lies from within, putting the *Hit Dog Hollering* from within on lockdown. In our *DIY Project*, when examining ourselves, it is best to be objective, forgiving, non-judgmental, honest, open, and focused.

With our *DIY Project*, we should not depend upon someone to do anything that we are not willing to do. Why? It breaks the mold of dependency on anyone outside of God. Plus, it challenges us; although this may require us to step outside, through, around, and over the box on a few things, it makes us multi-talented and valuable at the same time. There are times we must be willing to do what most are not willing to do.

Nevertheless, when you remove the limits on success, work hard, work with wisdom, do things differently, create strategies, and help others along the way, it will make you a RARE GEM that cannot be easily replaced in or out of the Kingdom of God.

Spiritual Tilling

When Spiritually Tilling your own ground, *As It Pleases God*, whether you are reaching beyond your self-imposed limitations or trusting God for your next, GREATNESS has your name on it, and it is your responsibility to knock, seek, and find. What does this mean? You must put in the WORK or TAKE ACTION for yourself. No one can do this for you but you! *"Ask, and it will be given to you; seek, and you will find; Knock and it will be opened to you. For everyone who asks receives, and he who seeks finds, and to him who knocks it will be opened."* Matthew 7:7-8.

Moreover, you have a choice of the Fruits you are bringing forth continuously. If you make a mistake or fall short, you should be quick to apologize or repent and even quicker to extend mercy and forgiveness.

Now, the question is, "What seeds are you planting?" Seeds of thought, seeds of action, seeds of reaction, seeds of deeds, and seeds of _____. Whatever it is, you fill in the blank on what is being sown in and out of season. Of course, everyone is sowing a seed for a different reason, purpose, or cause. My seed will not be the same as others because I am held to a higher accountability and penalty than someone who is just learning about the seeds that they are sowing.

For a surface seed to take root, one must water it! When we water a seed, it then begins to take root, growing into a habit that gives birth to the ROOT inside the seed. Once it is nurtured and it begins to grow, positively or negatively, what was once hidden beneath the surface will become exposed to others, bringing forth the Fruits after its kind.

What can fruits do for us? Unbeknown to most, they contain the cure or medicine for whatever we need. Let us take it to scripture: *"Behold, I will bring her healing and medicine, and I will* cure them and will reveal unto them the abundance of peace and truth." Jeremiah 33:6.

Our Abundance, Peace, and Truth of Life are in our Seeds. Most often, we downplay the significance of our Seeds, not realizing that everything has been birthed from some form of Seed. The Bible says, *"Behold, I have given you every plant yielding seed that is on the surface of all the earth, and every tree which has fruit yielding seed; it shall be food for you."* Genesis 1:29. Our character is no different. If there is a seed bearing the wrong fruit, we have the power to do something about it. According to Ecclesiastes 3:2, there is a *"time to plant and a time to uproot what is planted."*

Why do we need to uproot our seeds if they are already planted? Here is why, according to Deuteronomy 22:9: *"You shall not sow your vineyard with two kinds of seed, or all the produce of the seed which you have sown, and the increase of the vineyard will become defiled."* We must choose good or bad Seeds, positive or negative Seeds, right or wrong Seeds, etc. We cannot straddle the fence with our Seeds.

Most often, we focus on living our lives to the fullest, but we neglect the Principles of Justice, Compassion, Sharing, and Truth while doing our own thing. Just because it feels right, and we want what we want, does not necessarily mean that it is good for us or that it is right, *As It Pleases God*.

Chapter 5
Self-Talk

Everyone has a story to tell, regardless of whether we understand it or not. However, the first listener with *Self-Talk* takes place within ourselves. Throughout my journey in life, I have found that quite a few people do not really understand the difference between positive and negative self-talk, actions, reactions, thoughts, or behaviors. It is for this reason that I am opening the door for you to understand the difference between whether we are the *Hit Dog Hollering* or if it is within another. Why do we need to know the difference between the two? We do not want to become our worst enemy or the enemy of God.

Of course, many will laugh about this, but those are the ones who are aloof in their thinking, becoming, and doing, *As It Pleases God*, only to please themselves with a one-way ticket into the Pit with their mouths wide open and eyes sealed closed. More importantly, this is why the Bible says this about avoiding carnality: "*Set your mind on things above, not on things on the earth.*" Colossians 3:2.

When we have too much idle time to allow our minds and emotions to simmer with folly, it is a sign that we are not busy enough. When we become busy with positive, productive, and fruitful things, we have less time to entertain negative thoughts or emotions. Whether our *Self-Talk* is positive or negative, it will take place all the time, even when we want to turn the inner chatter off. Then again, most often, we drown it out with something else. Now, this is where our something else can deprive us from listening to ourselves, our instincts, conscience, or the red flags.

If you take a moment to think about your mindset, you will find that it likes to package things into a file cabinet with categories, labels, titles, and conditions. For the mind to do all of this, it has to isolate things, analyze them, and judge them, based on all the information that is currently available. This will also include your past experiences or mental conditioning process. Besides, if you have not noticed by now, the mind never shuts up; it is always commenting, analyzing, labeling, and separating.

The chatterbox mind also loves to entertain itself with the 'what if,' the 'if only,' the 'why didn't I,' and the 'I wish I had' questions or statements. Not only that, but you will find that your mind likes to nitpick and go over every incident, every experience, and especially every mistake you have ever made in your life. Then it thinks about the future, the things you have to do, the things you may have forgotten to do, and the things that may never happen. By far, this is exhausting! Moreover, please do not add in the 'I want,' the 'I hope,' and the 'I hope not' statements as well.

To add insult to injury, we start thinking or gossiping with others about what is going on, what went on in the past, and what could or would happen in the future. Unrelentingly, this is also where the NEWS comes in to brainwash us. And, we collectively start thinking about the victimization process of what other races, cultures, cities, states, and countries are doing as opposed to what we are doing, what we should be doing, what we are going to do, what we need to do, or what we are NOT doing. All of this goes on in our minds, all day long!

Then, we go to bed at night thinking about the same things that may or may not have anything to do with us. To add insult to another injury, the next day, we wake up with the same cycle without putting an end to yesterday's, the previous month's, or the previous year's events that may not even concern us or our well-being. It is a miracle that any of us can ever get anything done, with our minds going on and on about everything and everyone all of the time with unapologetic *Self-Talk*.

Our minds were designed to think, create, and order us around; however, we must understand we are in control of them and not allow them to control us. If we do not understand this, our minds will break us down in ways we could never reveal to anyone, affecting our behaviors, thoughts, beliefs, biases, fruits, and character. In alignment with our DNA, our minds are designed to build us up or break us down. By default, in conjunction with the psyche of mankind, it will choose to break us down naturally if we do not choose otherwise, positively. Know this: *"Many are the plans in a person's heart, but it is the Lord's purpose that prevails."* Proverbs 19:21.

Building or enhancing our *Self-Talk* is not a one-time choice; it is a moment-by-moment process. The mind is very strategic, and it is something we cannot see, taste, smell, hear, or touch, yet it is very powerful and obedient. Trust that the mind is always busy, either positively or negatively. We will never have to train our minds to do wrong—it comes naturally; however, we must train our minds to do what is right. The Bible tells us, *"Do not be conformed to this world, but be transformed by the renewing of your mind, that you may prove what is that good and acceptable and perfect will of God."* Romans 12:2.

According to the Heavenly of Heavens, our responsibility is to get ourselves to the point where we can ask ourselves the right questions. Why must we query ourselves as Believers? We must understand what to accept and what to cast down. If we are not asking the right questions or not querying at all, then how would we know if there is a stronghold or yoke attached to whatever with whomever? In the Spiritual Realm, we cannot assume...We must get the facts!

In taking querying a step further, we should not stop there. We must get an understanding of why we are doing what we do, why we are not doing what we need to do, what it is going to take to get us to where we need to be, how we are going to get there, and where we should go. What is the big deal, especially when it is just *Self-Talk*? Obedience to the Will of God is the deal. Here is what 2 Corinthians 10:3-5 says about this matter: *"For though we walk in the flesh, we do not war according to the flesh. For the weapons of our warfare are not carnal but mighty in God for pulling down strongholds, casting down arguments and every high thing that exalts itself against the knowledge of God, bringing every thought into captivity to the obedience of Christ."*

Our *Self-Talk* is the gateway into or out of the Kingdom, As It Pleases God. Really? Yes, really! Simply put, *"As he thinks in his heart, so is he. 'Eat and drink!' he says to you, But his heart is not with you."* Proverbs 23:7. Fortunately, this is one of the most well-known sayings, but it is also used the least in the Eye of God. The way we speak to ourselves when no one is looking is important because it is so easy to overlook, undermine, or underestimate the conversations we have with ourselves and about others.

After all, our internal dialogues shape our self-perception and influence our actions, words, desires, thoughts, and habits. But it also unveils our heart posture as well. Still, the question remains, 'Why are we in this condition, on the brink of collapse from the inside out?' Better yet, 'Why are we getting a side-eye from God, especially when we are more BLESSED than ever in the history of mankind?' 'Why are the *Hit Dogs Hollering* attempting to ruin the lives of others for fun?' Can we really make this make sense? How is the power of thought ruining our lives? Well, I will tell you... Let us get some ENTHUSIASM going.

Enthusiasm
Amid calmness lies a hidden secret called enthusiasm. It is a rare gem that is overlooked by most and used by few. However, in this book, *A Hit Dog Will Holler*, we must unveil it for a time such as this. Why? It helps us connect the dots to our Predestined Blueprinted Purpose.

For the record, the lack of enthusiasm does not mean that we cannot be happy, laugh, or smile; it means that we need to become excited. According to the Heavenly of Heavens, this is what gives us a GLOW or SPARKLE in our eyes. Believe it or not, enthusiasm is contagious! Being excited makes other people excited, and it gives them the courage to overcome and rebound as well. In addition, it will encourage them to seek out what we have or create a hunger to discover their Talents, Gifts, or Calling to experience their own bliss of enthusiasm.

Why should we use our Talents, Gifts, or Calling? As scripture says, "*Behold, I am coming quickly, and My reward is with Me, to give to every one according to his work.*" Revelation 22:12. With this being said, we have everything we need within us—all we need to do is gain access to it without caving ourselves into the *Hit Dog Hollering* mentality.

How do we gain access to enthusiasm, *As It Pleases God*? We must acknowledge the fact that it is there. Yet, inside of our enthusiasm lies our Creativity. Inside of our Creativity lies our Talents, Gifts, and Calling. Inside of our Talents, Gifts, and Calling lies our Vision. Inside of our Vision lies our Provision. Inside of our Provision lies our Divine Destiny. Inside of our Destiny lies our Divine Favor and Protection. What a connection, right?

A Hit Dog Can Holler all it wants, but you still have what it takes to get the job done, *As It Pleases God*. Move forward in the Spirit of Excellence, doing what you were called to do!

Chapter 6
Self-Awareness

Now that we have our minds right from the previous chapter, let us change gears for a moment. Our lives are a personal reflection of who we are, and the Essence of our *Self-Awareness* has nothing to do with thinking and everything to do with BEING! It is the "IS" phase or the "I AM" phase of who we are, which creates our uniqueness. It is all about being ourselves fully and embracing that oneness with life as we do our part in creating a better place, and recognizing our vulnerabilities and shortcomings.

In this busy world of today, everything is rush-rush, so much so that our minds do not have time to catch up or reflect. As a result, we suffer from the *Hit Dog* and *Hollering* mentality. Due to this oversight or lack of understanding, great ideas, thoughts, and inspirations regarding our Predestined Blueprint get lost in the shuffle. As the scriptures state: "*My people are destroyed for lack of knowledge.*" Hosea 4:6.

What if we do not need to become Self-Aware? Please do not be deceived. It is intertwined in our DNA. Thus, we all need it, even if we pretend we do not. Why? We are Spiritual Beings having a human experience and are in need of a Spiritual Mirror to see the unseen. If not, the enemy gains leverage over our inadequacies and denials, causing *A Hit Dog To Holler* loudly.

It is as real as Spiritual Warfare, Spiritual Oppression, Spiritual Exclusion, or Spiritual Deception. If we think for a moment that we are exempt from this form of Spiritual Paralysis, think again. Listen, we are a SPIRIT first and foremost, living in a body that has a soul with a mind to think. If we think for a moment that we can bypass the SPIRIT, we are mistaken again. *"For anyone who hears the word but does not carry it out is like a man who looks at his face in a mirror, and after observing himself goes away and immediately forgets what he looks like."* James 1:23-24.

A Hit Dog Will Holler is limited in its reach and Spiritual Capacity, *As It Pleases God*. Nevertheless, remember that anyone can experience the impact of a *Hit Dog*. Why? It is a result of being Spiritually Blind, Spiritually Deaf, or Spiritually Mute; therefore, they do not care how their behaviors, thoughts, words, or beliefs impact those around them. As a result, they continue with their antics as if they are God's gift to humanity.

Although our Spirit will lie dormant until we awaken it, do not ever think we are of our own. When our Spirit is asleep, so are we in the Spiritual Realm, therefore producing the onset of the ailments leading to our Spiritual Paralysis, causing *A Hit Dog To Holler* by allowing certain things to occur. Here are a few examples of this condition in real-time:

- ☐ When we begin to read the Bible, we get sleepy.
- ☐ When our emotions are high, we are not able to control them, and we tend to forget our home training.

- ☐ When we become angry, we tend to forget about Godly Character.
- ☐ When we are not interested in the Sunday sermon, our mind wanders off.
- ☐ When we are faced with the lust of the flesh, the lust of the eyes, or the pride of life, we tend to forget what the Bible says about self-control.
- ☐ When we receive great advice regarding our issues in life, we do not take heed.
- ☐ When we are hurt, we tend to seek revenge, blocking out all the good we saw at the beginning of the relationship.
- ☐ When we have trust issues, our minds will create all types of untrue or fictitious scenarios.
- ☐ When someone has been proven to do good, yet with one mistake, we forget about all of the good they have contributed to our lives in a fraction of a second.
- ☐ When we are in a fight, we go for the jugular vein without exercising our ability to walk away in peace or de-escalate the situation.
- ☐ When we are designed to unite, we allow envy, jealousy, and coveting to divide us through our own selfish ambitions.
- ☐ When we are designed to live in harmony, we allow unresolved discord to put a monkey wrench in our efforts.
- ☐ When we are designed to forgive, instead, we hold on to the unforgiveness, revenge, or hate, giving us an excuse to remain upset, hurt, or deceived.
- ☐ When we break up or get divorced, we tend to forget about the love we proclaimed to have for that individual as we secretly seek their demise.

Before I move on, let me align this with scripture: *"The person without the Spirit does not accept the things that come from the Spirit of God but considers them foolishness, and cannot understand them."* 1 Corinthians 2:14.

The *Hit Dog Hollering* is nothing to play around with; it will zap our thoughts and creativity faster than light. Plus, it will cause us to second-guess ourselves, then cause us to become full of doubt and negativity, without us realizing what is taking place until it is brought to our attention, or we do not know who we have become.

As I move on, my next question is, 'Do you like who you see in the mirror?' In this dog-eat-dog or *Hit Dog* world, this is another question that must be answered. If one has not noticed, as a majority, we have a history of not being satisfied with who we are. If we have curly hair, we want straight hair. If we have brown eyes, we then desire another color, and the list goes on.

Listen, fake facades cannot last forever; we will get tired, and our true colors will come forth in due time. Therefore, if we become grateful for who we are, it simplifies our lives; plus, we will have more time to work on our inner qualities of genuineness. What is the purpose of knowing this? The *Hit Dog* will capitalize on our insecurities, attempting to force change with our physical features to please them.

Self-appreciation and gratefulness give us the ability to get in the Spirit to value ourselves positively while inspiring others to do likewise. Furthermore, it helps us to develop and maintain the 3 P's: Purpose, Passion, and Perseverance. How do we obtain the 3 P's? I would say it is through humility. I know it seems far-fetched, but it is the truth. When we are humble, we are able to listen, learn, do, and share on a level that will get us heard.

Those who talk too much do not really get heard much. It is those who say less and do more that really get heard. It is said that action speaks louder than words; well, now we know why! People are more willing to help us when we are not a know-it-all, when we are kind, when we are patient, when we are transparent, and when we ask the right questions.

As life progresses in a forward motion, and everyone is out for themselves, some of the superficial teachings tend to lead us further and further away from who we are, how we were created, and what we were created to do. In my opinion, this keeps us distracted with the issues of life, current worldly news, materialism, coveting, and keeping up with the Joneses. It is the issues and traumas of life that cause many of us to question our purpose, our mission, our mentors, and God.

Now, let me ask a question: 'Why would we have been put on earth if we were not supposed to be here, do something, or make some form of impact?' Typically, this is indeed a common question for most of those who are struggling with embracing the full impact of their uniqueness or gifting. Once we get to this point of questioning, regardless of how much we try to block it out, it will arise in our minds constantly as a reminder or an alarm, letting us know we must WAKE UP!

Our *Self-Awareness* is about living now while we are here. And we never want to put ourselves into the *Hit Dog Will Holler* category. With this being said, right now is the time to GET UP, make our MARK or IMPACT. Trust me, there is no way around this, especially if you are reading this book—the calling is so strong in your life. You can fight your calling all you want, but in the wee hours of the night, His Voice will call, and you will eventually answer; it is just a matter of time. God is working on the OBEDIENCE of the masses; therefore, you must step up or step down!

Obedience

Obedience is the one word that causes most people to cringe when it is indeed one of the most powerful attributes known to man. Most often, we fall into bondage due to the lack of obedience to God, ourselves, and others. Let me say this before I move on, 'Our freedom is tied to our willingness to obedience.'

Let us take obedience back to the Garden of Eden, where Adam and Eve were put out of the Garden due to their disobedience. Some would argue that it was Eve's disobedience that caused them to be put out of the Garden, and they are partially correct. But it was Adam's disobedience as well...God gave Adam the instructions not to partake of the Tree of Good and Evil. Of course, he relayed that message to Eve, but in his ignorance, he took a bite of the Forbidden Fruit as well.

Just because someone is exhibiting disobedience, why would we follow them? You got it! Emotional soul ties will cause us to follow others into the abyss due to the fear of loss, loneliness, or acceptance.

In my opinion, if Adam had not taken a bite of the Forbidden Fruit, we would not be experiencing the struggles we face today. I am not here to blame Adam; I am only here to drive obedience back home to where it belonged in the first place. If Adam had only stood his ground on being obedient, God would have dealt with Eve.

Nonetheless, they both took a bite of the Forbidden Fruit, and they both resorted to the blaming game. Is this not what we are still doing today? We partake of people, places, and things that are not good for us, and when we get caught up, we point the finger, laying the blame on something, someone, or our past!

Some would say, 'If God knew that Adam and Eve would eat from the Tree of Good and Evil, why would he place it there?' He placed it there to give us a CHOICE. The fascinating aspect of human life is having FREE WILL. The free will to choose...if we lose our Power of Choice, we are no more than a mere robot.

Not only do we have free will, but we also have emotions that are beyond human comprehension. In my opinion, God may not have added that into the equation when he introduced Eve into Adam's life. If one does not believe this, why would God curse the woman in Genesis 3:16, saying, "*I will greatly multiply your sorrow and your conception; In pain you shall bring forth children; Your desire will be for your husband, and he will rule over you.*"

We can debate whether or not it is a curse, or a play on words...It is indeed a Spiritual Yoke of Disobedience that cannot be reversed. Based on the Spiritual Law of Duality that Adam and Eve willfully invoked, it is not easy to give birth, raise a child, or satisfy our husbands without God Almighty. And for a woman who says it is without Him is a liar. Yes, I said it! It takes work, and if we do not want to put in the work, do not give birth, do not have children, and do not get married. And by golly, do not do any of them if we fail to work on ourselves to become better, stronger, and wiser, *As It Pleases God* with a work-in-progress mindset.

Let us get back to the story: God knew at that point in the garden or the game with Adam and Eve, that the woman ruled over the male, and He put a stop to that. How so? Adam made a conscious choice to forfeit the Garden of Eden to suffer death with Eve. Was he Emotionally, Physically, or Mentally caught up? He was definitely not Spiritually caught up; he willingly sacrificed everything not to feel the sting of loneliness again. As a result of this particular downfall, God reversed the role of emotions with the male population because Adam got caught up in his emotions.

Let me clear the air: Men and women are both still emotional, but men can control or cover up their emotions better than women. When a woman controls or tries to control the household, most often, he will secretly or openly rebel against her, which sometimes results in emotional, mental, physical, and the blaming game of abuse. Unfortunately, this is where the tit-for-tat games come into play, driving our divorce rate up to a whopping 80% failure rate.

When a man cannot listen to his woman, and when a woman cannot listen to her man, there is a big problem. A communication problem, to be exact! This problem must be resolved as soon as possible because once the communication is gone, then the emotions will be lost. Once the emotions are gone, then goes the mind. Once someone is mentally gone in a relationship, it is only a matter of time before the body will physically move on.

On the other side of obedience, there will be the lack of it, which leaves room for the Spirit of Rebellion to take up residence. A rebellious individual constitutes someone who does not like to be told what to do. We will find that this type of person will have run-ins with the law, will go from job to job, be very disrespectful, extremely confrontational, angry, rude, or hateful, use foul language, and be very insensitive with their words.

Amid all this, this does not make a person a bad person; it simply makes them misunderstood, which feeds, fuels, and justifies their stance in disobedience, making them a prime candidate for the *Hit Dog The Will Holler*. Keep in mind that where there is disobedience, there will also be a state of confusion that will reside from within the individual, then extend its way out into the physical aspects of life. When one sees a certain level of irresponsibility, exercise extreme caution. Why? The *Hit Dog's* genderless personality will eventually make us holler!

Regardless of where we are or who we are, we are all in need of some form of healing, *As It Pleases God*. If we deny this need,

Self-Awareness becomes blurred and smeared in the lives of others. How do we blur the lines in this matter? We begin to live a lie, ushering ourselves into a phase of crushing our stones with bad habits or addictions, as opposed to learning and building ourselves up from the inside out, *As It Pleases Him.*

Chapter 7

People Skills

Our *People Skills* are all about promoting excellent communication and building better relationships, *As It Pleases God*. There are certain things money cannot buy, and CHARACTER is one of them, even if we are groomed with proper etiquette. What we will find is that a lot of people talk the talk but do not walk the walk, especially behind closed doors. In this book, I will share with you how to walk the walk and talk the talk naturally with no strings attached!

Life is not a bed of roses; however, you can decide on your approach to your bed of roses. You can decide the color, the location, how to decorate the rose bed, the nutrients, when to water them, etc. Let your imagination go to work for you...I am living proof of how to take negatives and turn them into positives based on the information I feed myself and what I am now feeding you. Rest assured, I am not feeding you fluff...If you work on yourself with a work-in-progress mentality, *As It Pleases God* with the Fruits of the Spirit in hand, He will help you develop impeccable *People Skills*, GUARANTEED!

In the Eye of God, exceptional *People Skills* are not just about being polite and courteous to others. It is about living out our faith in every aspect of our lives, including how we interact with others, *As It Pleases Him*.

Exceptional *People Skills* involve being empathetic, compassionate, patient, and understanding towards others. It also means being able to listen to others attentively without interrupting them or responding prematurely. In the Eye of God, it involves putting ourselves in others' shoes and seeing things from their perspective.

As Believers, we are called to love our neighbors as ourselves, regardless of their race, ethnicity, idiosyncrasies, social status, or whatever. It involves being honest and transparent in our dealings with others, communicating our thoughts and opinions tactfully, without being rude, insensitive, or offensive.

In addition, exceptional *People Skills* involve being able to work well in a team to collaborate with others towards a common goal and finding common ground, even when we have different opinions, ideas, thoughts, and beliefs.

How do we make our *People Skills* make sense, *As It Pleases God*? For example, Molly has always been known for her exceptional *People Skills*. She had a way of making even the most difficult people feel wanted, heard, loved, and understood by using the Fruits of the Spirit consistently. And it was this skill that brought Buddy into her life.

Buddy was a really rough-around-the-edge kind of guy with a southern twang who had a gruff demeanor and a reputation for being difficult to work with. For this reason, people often made fun of him for his differences, causing him to react unfavorably. However, when he was assigned to work with Molly on a project, he did not know anything about her; however, he did expect her to be like all of his other coworkers.

From day one, Molly treated Buddy with kindness and respect. She listened to his ideas without dismissing them, even when they were different from her own. She asked him questions and took an interest in his life outside of work, building an excellent rapport.

Slowly but surely, Buddy began to open up to Molly as he talked about his past and the present struggles he faced. Molly listened without judgment or criticism, offering words of encouragement and support while thanking him for sharing his story.

As their project progressed, Buddy began to see the world differently, realizing everyone was not out to get him, as Molly's kindness and compassion profoundly impacted him. And it was not long before he began to ask her about her beliefs.

Molly was a devout Christian, and she did not shy away from sharing her faith with others. She told Buddy about the love of God and how it had changed her life as he listened, becoming more intrigued by her words.

Over time, he asked more questions as his curiosity increased, wanting to learn more about the God she served. Eventually, he attended service with Molly and came into a personal relationship with God for himself. Looking back, Buddy knew that it was Molly's exceptional *People Skills* that helped save him from himself. Her kindness and compassion had opened his heart to the love of God. Above all, he was grateful for her friendship and guidance because he had never experienced a friend who was on the give instead of on the take.

Molly, for her part, was humbled and grateful to have played a small part in Buddy's journey. She knew that it was God who had worked in his heart, but she was glad that God used her to be the vessel to develop a solid relationship with a lifelong friend. Because she, too, was once rough around the edges, and

God smoothed her out to create smooth sailing relationships with others, *As It Pleased Him*.

When exemplifying your *People Skills*, as long as you own your truth, ask yourself the right questions, develop a system for yourself, and exhibit the Fruits of the Spirit, *As It Pleases God*, you CANNOT lose on this journey. I am giving you the information you need to pierce the bottled-up CREATIVITY that has been longing to come forth. All I need you to do is run your own race and refuse to player hate, covet others with the superficial *Hole in the Bucket* persona, or allow the *Hit Dog Hollering* to distract you. Here are a few tips on developing your *People Skills*, but not limited to such:

- ☐ Practice active listening in conversation.
- ☐ Develop empathy towards others.
- ☐ Respect others' opinions and perspectives.
- ☐ Keep an open mind when meeting new people.
- ☐ Learn to read nonverbal cues.
- ☐ Maintain good eye contact and nod often.
- ☐ Speak clearly and confidently.
- ☐ Show appreciation and gratitude.
- ☐ Avoid interrupting others.
- ☐ Be approachable and friendly.
- ☐ Give and receive constructive feedback.
- ☐ Keep your promises and commitments.
- ☐ Be patient and understanding.
- ☐ Develop conflict resolution skills.
- ☐ Be a good team player.
- ☐ Avoid gossip and negativity.
- ☐ Keep conversations positive.
- ☐ Develop your sense of humor.
- ☐ Be willing to admit mistakes.
- ☐ Strive for continuous self-improvement.

What are the indications that we need to work on our *People Skills*? Listed below are a few indicators, but not limited to such:

- ☐ When we are always complaining about something or someone.
- ☐ When we are focused on what is wrong instead of what is right.
- ☐ When we do not like people.
- ☐ When we are easily offended.
- ☐ When we negatively gossip about others.
- ☐ When we have a hard time accepting responsibility for our actions.
- ☐ When we are quick to judge others.
- ☐ When we rarely have anything positive to say.
- ☐ When we have a hard time being happy for others.
- ☐ When we blame others for our problems.
- ☐ When we do not seem to have any goals or ambitions.
- ☐ When we are always negative.
- ☐ When we are pessimistic about the future.
- ☐ When we have a hard time being kind to others.
- ☐ When we have a hard time seeing the good in others.
- ☐ When we are always critical of others.
- ☐ When we do not seem to have any hobbies or interests.
- ☐ When we are easily frustrated.

Chapter 8
A Hit Dog Will Holler

The southern proverb, '*A Hit Dog Will Holler*,' is loaded with Divine Wisdom, *As It Pleases God*. It teaches us how to deal with those who are different or challenging to deal with. Regardless of how we look at ourselves, how we look at our lives, or where we are from, our roots are who we are! It is our ancestry, it is our legacy, it is our background, and it is our lifeline, whether we acknowledge or deny it. More importantly, we should never allow our persona to become that of a *Hit Dog*.

What will cause *A Hit Dog To Holler*? Everyone is different, with varying traumas, triggers, and conditioning. So, I cannot pinpoint the cause without having the opportunity to set my Spiritual Eyes on the person, to listen with my Spiritual Ears, or being able to speak with my Spiritual Voice with the utterance from the Spirit of the Living God. Therefore, we are going to use roundabout Spiritual Principles, Laws, and Concepts to tame the *Hit Dog* from within or in our vicinity.

Just remember, the same *Hit Dog* that surrounds us is within us as well...thus, it must be TAMED, *As It Pleases God*. What does this mean in layman's terms? The *Hit Dog* is a character trait that we must deal with by exhibiting the Fruits of the Spirit while allowing the most dominant fruit of SELF-CONTROL to lead the others. Without it, playing cleanup will become our portion as we lose the credibility and trust of those around us.

Nevertheless, once we develop a *Spirit to Spirit* Relationship with God, He will lift the veil from our eyes, unclog our ears, and speak through us in ways that will blow our minds, helping us to deal with *A Hit Dog* or whether the *Hit Dog* is within us. Really? Yes, really! What if we do not have this characteristic? Unfortunately, we all have some form of resounding trauma hidden within, called a trigger. Once the trigger is pushed, *The Hit Dog Will Holler!* The secret is knowing how to reel it in quickly, succinctly, and professionally, *As It Pleases God*.

If one has not noticed, our veins are similar to the roots of a tree or plant, which are considered the lifeline of anything living. Listen, the fruits we bear come from within; therefore, we must get a good understanding of the ROOT. The root cause, the root reason, or the core of our issues are hidden in plain sight, which happens to have the answers within the depths of our souls. As scripture has it, "*Out of the abundance of the heart the mouth speaks,*" Matthew 12:34.

When we deny or hide our roots, it brings about a form of inner sickness or insecurities. Unfortunately, this is what drives us to pretend as if we are more than we are. It also causes us to deny the true essence of why we are here, as well as what brought us to this point in our lives. When we take on a form of pretense or denial, it keeps our passions hidden or neglected. Once this happens, we will find that we will develop an inferiority complex when dealing with others, a sense of paranoia, or a judgmental spirit that condemns others, as opposed to building, mentoring, and sharing.

A *Hit Dog Will Holler* when the door is opened on their hidden inferiority complex. How do we make this make sense? An inferiority complex is a psychological condition characterized by feelings of inadequacy, self-doubt, and a lack of self-worth that no one is exempt from due to an underlying weakness. Frankly, this is the reason for becoming a work-in-progress, *As It Pleases God*. If we opt to ignore this complex, leaving it hidden or as-is, it will make us feel anxious, insecure, unmotivated, resistant, or even depressed.

When we pretend and fake as if we are perfect, think we are better than others, or compare ourselves, we become a prime target of UNEASE in the Eye of God. Really? Yes, really! The lies we feed our psyche keep records, setting a trap for us. And the moment we desire to break free of its chokehold, it will fight us back, bringing all of our LIES, SEEDS, and DEEDS to the forefront (To Mind) as leverage or justification with a mental playback or movie reel in our Mind's Eye. Is this humanly possible? Absolutely. All we need to do is check our thoughts, mental chatter, or self-talk, which is enough to make any *Hit Dog Holler*!

What would cause the *Hit Dog* complex to happen to us or penetrate, especially as Believers covered by the Blood of Jesus? Even if we cover ourselves with the Blood of Jesus or proclaim Holiness, it cannot cover what we refuse to deal with or what we pretend does not exist. More importantly, we cannot use coming to Christ as an excuse not to work on ourselves to become better, stronger, and wiser, *As It Pleases God*. We must understand the underlying ROOT of whatever, whomever, and whyever.

Besides, pleading the Blood of Jesus over other people while refusing to plead the Blood over ourselves and our issues creates

Spiritual Violations in or out of the Kingdom of God. Is this Biblical? I would have it no other way! *"And why do you look at the speck in your brother's eye, but do not consider the plank in your own eye? Or how can you say to your brother, 'Let me remove the speck from your eye'; and look, a plank is in your own eye? Hypocrite! First remove the plank from your own eye, and then you will see clearly to remove the speck from your brother's eye."* Matthew 7:3-5. Here are a few causes for the *Hit Dog* complex, but not limited to such:

- ☐ Childhood experiences of criticism.
- ☐ Continuous neglect.
- ☐ Traumatic experiences such as bullying or abuse.
- ☐ Comparison to peers or siblings.
- ☐ Physical appearance or disabilities.
- ☐ Social status or economic background.
- ☐ Lack of achievement or success.
- ☐ Academic or professional challenges.
- ☐ Fear of failure or rejection.
- ☐ Cultural or societal expectations.
- ☐ Parental or family pressure.
- ☐ Past negative experiences.
- ☐ Negative self-talk or beliefs.
- ☐ Perfectionism.
- ☐ Lack of self-care or self-esteem.
- ☐ Chronic stress or anxiety.
- ☐ Introversion or shyness.
- ☐ Relationship issues or breakups.
- ☐ Health issues or chronic illnesses.
- ☐ Aging or changes in physical ability.
- ☐ Unmet needs or goals.

Is it better to leave well enough alone? It depends on the situation, circumstance, or event; however, our well enough may not be God's well enough. We must determine if we are dealing with avoidance or healing. In the Eye of God, we do not have to confront others or become confrontational to work on ourselves, *As It Pleases Him*.

The most confident and successful people experience self-doubt, challenges, and reservations just like those who appear or feel unsuccessful. However, it only becomes an issue if we do not develop a work-in-progress mentality, *As It Pleases God*, our perception is selfishly keeled, or when leading in the wrong field, contradicting our Divine Blueprint.

Whether we are at the top or bottom of our game, we must know what to do, why we are doing so, how to do it, where to engage, and with whom, *As It Pleases God* with self-compassion. All this means is that we must acknowledge our mistakes, idiosyncrasies, and limitations without judgment and focus on our strengths and positive qualities, *As It Pleases Him*. While at the same time, keeping everything moving in the Spirit of Excellence, giving and doing our best, even if we are not perfect.

On the other hand, if we are clueless about these factors and deadset on pleasing ourselves, going from pillar to post, we will find the *Hit Dog Will Holler* to no avail, regardless of who we are, why we are, where we are, or what we have going on.

According to the Heavenly of Heavens, we must Spiritually Till our own ground and take action towards our goals using what we have in our hands, even if we feel unsure or inadequate. By stepping out of our comfort zone and taking risks, we can build resilience and confidence in our abilities. Even if we do not achieve our desired outcome or fail, we can LEARN from the experience and use it as an opportunity for growth, primarily if we document our journey and add God into our equational efforts.

Let us explore some ways to help feel more grounded and at ease, *As It Pleases God*, and overcome the *Hit Dog* complex. What is the purpose of understanding this? All the money in the world cannot stop this complex, mainly if we do not deal with it, *As It Pleases Him*. Why? It places a YOKE on the human psyche with our permission. How is this possible? With the human psyche, the omission is indeed PERMISSION. Listed below are a few ways, but not limited to such:

- ☐ Recognize and accept your feelings of inferiority.
- ☐ Identify the root cause of your inferiority complex.
- ☐ Challenge or counteract negative self-talk with positivity.
- ☐ Use positive affirmations.
- ☐ Focus on your strengths and accomplishments.
- ☐ Surround yourself with positive and supportive people.
- ☐ Set realistic goals.
- ☐ Become grateful for everything.
- ☐ Learn new skills and challenge yourself.
- ☐ Avoid comparing yourself to others.
- ☐ Take responsibility for your own happiness and success.
- ☐ Learn to communicate your needs effectively.
- ☐ Practice forgiveness and repentance.
- ☐ Let go of past mistakes and failures by extracting the lesson.
- ☐ Embrace imperfections and focus on self-improvement.
- ☐ Cultivate a positive mindset and attitude.
- ☐ Keep a journal.
- ☐ Use the Fruits of the Spirit and behave Christlike.
- ☐ Add God into the equational efforts of all things, even if you do not understand it, them, or that.
- ☐ Exhibit RESPECT, period.

Respectfulness

When it comes down to respect...we must give it to get it. There are times when we live by a double standard, where we demand respect from others without being a respectful person. Nevertheless, when dealing with taming the *Hit Dog* from within, respectfulness is a prerequisite. Why? *"If a wise man contends with a foolish man, Whether the fool rages or laughs, there is no peace."* Proverbs 29:9.

In the Eye of God, we must avoid becoming argumentative. What does God have to do with whether we argue or not, and we have free will to say whatever, whenever, however, and with whomever? *"Better to dwell in a corner of a housetop, than in a house shared with a contentious woman."* Proverbs 21:9. Well, what about men? Simply put, it takes two to tango... *"But avoid foolish and ignorant disputes, knowing that they generate strife."* 2 Timothy 2:23.

If someone wants to pick a fight, we do not have to respond. *"Do not answer a fool according to his folly, Lest you also be like him."* Proverbs 26:4. Nonetheless, if we are guilty of something, admit it, apologize for it, acquit it, and move on. Although it may not be easy all the time; however, it does work 80% of the time. Time is too precious to get caught up in arguing about people, places, and things we cannot change. Therefore, *"Let your speech always be with grace, seasoned with salt, that you may know how you ought to answer each one."* Colossians 4:6.

Always remember, everyone has an opinion. Even though a person is entitled to their opinion, it does not mean we have to agree or disagree. What it does mean is that we have the right to remain neutral. *"Even a fool is counted wise when he holds his peace; When he shuts his lips, he is considered perceptive."* Proverbs 17:28.

Besides, our level of respect does not give us the right to shut people down or mistreat them based on what they believe or how they think. Our responsibility is to align ourselves and our Bloodline, *As It Pleases God*, and then spread outwardly with the Fruits of the Spirit with the heart posture like: "*As for me and my house, we will serve the Lord.*" Joshua 24:15. By far, it helps us to become a living example, beginning with our homes first.

Here is an example: Avoid saying, 'You are wrong,' if you do not agree with something. Simply say, 'You are entitled to your own opinion,' or 'I respect your opinion,' and leave it alone, remaining Loveable, Joyful, Peaceful, Patient, Kind, Good, Gentle, Faithful, Gentle, and exhibiting Self-Control.

When respectfully leading our field in the Spirit of Excellence and *As It Pleases God*, the elements of praise have a profound way of getting the attention of those who would typically put up a mental or emotional wall. When providing feedback, it is always best to use ourselves as an example because we are all subjected to error on occasion. People will feel comfortable with those who own their mistakes and use them as a learning tool to build others, as opposed to bringing them down, making them feel bad, or making them feel as if they cannot get anything right.

Throughout my journey, I have found that perfection is a perceptional illusion because growth is a part of life. We grow up, we grow into, we grow through, and we grow out of people, places, and things. Without any form of growth, people, places, and things will begin to deteriorate; therefore, it is a great option to offer positive criticism in the form of a question. It will get our wheels turning with ourselves and in the lives of others. Why? In all simplicity, I am Dr. Y. for a reason, and the best way to solve a problem or to get answers is to ask the right questions, *As It Pleases God*.

Querying for selfish or manipulative reasons can get us caught up or blocked. How can we get blocked or caught up when doing our due diligence as Believers? When we do not know what or who we are dealing with or how God is using or training them, we can overstep our boundaries due to the lack of Spiritual Discernment.

The moment we think we have all the answers without exercising Spiritual Discernment, our Inner Genius will stop providing information to us. As a result, we begin making up stuff out of the blue and spewing foolery, appearing correct but untrue in the Eye of God. The bottom line is that it is not how much we know; it is how well we use, understand, discern, and apply what we know correctly. It is through our ability to listen, learn, extract, convert, grow, utilize, and share that we can bring about the WISDOM we all seek, *As It Pleases God*.

In all honesty, I have not met anyone who does not have the desire to become wise...we all want it. Most of us do not believe we have it or deserve it when it is indeed already embedded in our DNA. All we need to do is learn how to tap into the ROOT of it, *As It Pleases God!* Why must we add Him to the equation? We have a choice between lowercase wisdom or uppercase Divine Wisdom. Which would you prefer?

By accepting Divine Wisdom, *As It Pleases God*, we are better able to truly face the issues of life without having to lie to ourselves. Not only that, we are better able to prepare for the good and bad without having to worry about what we cannot change. In the Eye of God, this also gives us the opportunity to own our truth by making positive assessments, getting all the facts, narrowing down the problem, finding the root causes of our issues, or making positive improvements to uproot or prune the people, places, and things that have the potential to stunt our growth.

We will find that once the element of respect is genuinely established from within the core of our being, *As It Pleases God*, we will be more at peace with our decisions. If we dare to stand up or stand down for ourselves in this manner, we will find our faith becoming stronger, giving us an element of hope that is beyond human understanding.

Plus, if we add a little gratefulness into our respectfulness, we will find that favor and blessings will begin to follow us in ways that winning becomes an expectation, even in the midst of what may appear to be a failure to others. When one is able to look for the good in all things, one is well on their way to honing in on the Inner Genius mentality. Once this happens, our Genius from within will put us in a league of our own, where we do not have to compare ourselves to others, put down others to build ourselves up, or become a *Hit Dog Hollering*.

We are all gifted...once we learn how to RESPECT ourselves and others, our CREATIVITY will show up in areas where we may have been defeated. No one knows outside of the Holy Trinity how it is going to reveal itself. Nevertheless, one must be ready, willing, and able to step up to the plate, or it may require us to step down.

Similar to a *Hit Dog*, our Inner Genius is not anything to play around with. When our giftings yield to us, we must own them! If one is not able to own their past or where they are from, then they are NOT ready.

The Bible is full of stories, and so are we...once those lessons or journeys are called upon to inspire others, it becomes a TESTAMENT! Here is the catch...it can be positive or negative. I suggest that one should keep their Testaments on the positive side of the spectrum because here again, our Testaments are Seeds that will bear fruit after their own kind.

Our Testimony is a ROOT that has an Inner-bred Genius attached to it. If one has a hard time believing this, look at the roots of any plant; there will always be one root that is bigger than any other root. If that root is removed, the plant will die a slow death because the other roots can only sustain it for a certain amount of time. The same applies to us...our roots can only nourish us for a certain amount of time if we do not bring forth our Inner Genius. Once this happens, from within, our *Hit Dog Will Holler* to get our attention, or any type of attention, good, bad, or indifferent.

Dying a slow death from the inside out is the worst feeling one can ever endure. What causes a slow death from the inside out? I am so glad you asked. It is fear, anger, resentment, hatred, unforgiveness, guilt, jealousy, envy, worry, arrogance, cruelness, laziness, greediness, ungratefulness, paranoia, selfishness, vindictiveness, violence, plotting wickedness, slander of the innocent, disrespectfulness, a trouble-maker, or a *Hit Dog* recruiting *Hit Puppies*, making them holler. All in all, it is our character that determines the fruit we bear.

Chapter 9
Overcome Distractions

Before God created man, He prepared everything for us to enjoy. He did not create us to be condescending with our wants, needs, and desires. He definitely did not want things to overshadow Him, distract us, cause us to become *Hit Dogs Hollering*, or for us to idolize ourselves just because we have dominion, money, power, fame, fortune, status, or followers. However, in His All-knowing Eye, the best way we can ever *Overcome Distractions* is to be fully present in the moment to recognize it for what it is, as opposed to being fully absent as if it does not exist. Here is what is required of us: "*Put to death, therefore, whatever belongs to your earthly nature, sexual immorality, impurity, lust, evil desires and greed, which is idolatry.*" Colossians 3:5.

Since the wave of social media, we act as if we do not have any home training in public. We have lost respect for our elders, exhibiting defiant behavior in our homes, selling our souls at the drop of a dime, etc. Name it, it is happening...but, where do we go from here? Well, I will tell you...We need to go UP, *As It Pleases God!*

Since the downfall of man, we have been fighting a hidden battle from within for a long time. Well, now is the time to restore the bond that was lost in the Garden of Eden. The long-awaited relationship is for the taking, and I am going to give you the SECRETS on how to get it.

To begin, you are restored every morning that you wake up; all you need to do is to bring all your focus and awareness to the present moment by giving THANKS and RESPECT. It does not matter what is going on in your life right now...whether it is good, bad, pleasant, unpleasant, positive, negative, exciting, or boring, give THANKS.

Your psyche will continue to try to distract you by labeling, analyzing, and judging you to create a bed of doubt or distraction to steal your ability to live a peaceful lifestyle. Nevertheless, to *Overcome Distractions*, you must embrace inner joy, experience love, be patient, exhibit self-control, be kind to others, do good, be gentle, and most of all, be faithful.

The beginning of *Overcoming Distractions* is in the acceptance of the Fruits of the Spirit. Can it be this simple? Yes and no! Yes, it can be this simple, and you must say 'NO' to a lot of people, places, and things that are not conducive. Sometimes, it may hurt, or it may require you to be alone. It is a give-and-take situation you must be ready for.

The *Overcoming* process is often downplayed by those who do not understand its power. As I speak directly to you, you cannot solve a problem if you cannot see the problem for what it really is. If your mind and ego are busy trying to distract you, you will never fully see what is in front of you. As a result, you will often find yourself reacting in anger, disgust, fear, or other negative emotions that deplete your power, causing you to become a *Hit Dog Hollering* or *Hit Dog Whimpering* because you cannot have your way.

The behaviors motivated by negative emotions will only create more problems for you by revoking your right to be Spiritual at that moment. It is for this reason that I want you to stay in the present, checking your emotions to ensure that you are exhibiting the Fruits of the Spirit, *As It Pleases God*. The very moment you are stepping away from the Fruits of the Spirit, you can make the immediate corrections necessary to bring yourself back into alignment. Doing so helps bring forth the clarity needed to readjust your mindset or ego-set to ensure you make wise decisions or take action if necessary.

On the flip side of things, when you conflict with yourself, you will attract unnecessary drama, problems, or unexplained suffering. Then again, it sometimes may cause an identity crisis. But let me say this: Conflict has no power over you unless you give it the power! Therefore, it is always best to squash the superficial ego and control your mind to prevent unnecessary Spiritual Warfare from within the depths of your soul. In the Eye of God, this will ensure your Inner Genius stands out among the crowd with no shame attached, ushering you into your NEXT.

The Antidote

The longing for a Spiritual Relationship, the longing to be in Purpose on purpose, and the longing to use our giftings and talents do not go away; they get stronger, persistent, and demanding. Depending upon how strong the calling is, there are times when our Divine Purpose will not allow us to have peace. There are also times when the pressures of life get us to the point where things do not matter anymore, as Divine

Purpose becomes the sought-after antidote, the Spiritual Antidote, to be exact.

Is it possible to be Spiritually Hassled for the Spiritual Antidote? The answer is 'Yes.' I am pretty sure you have heard the scripture, "*Many are called, and few are chosen.*" Matthew 22:14. When a person is Divinely Chosen for a specific Predestined Purpose, the issues of life will drive them toward that Spiritual Antidote with a battle between pursuing *As It Pleases God* or giving up to please ourselves. Thus, sparking an ongoing struggle with our faith and hope, determining the MANY from the FEW.

Some will fight tooth and nail to avoid the Spiritual Calling, as I did at one point, but I eventually surrendered to the Divine Calling from my Heavenly Father. Although I did not understand it at first, I came forth kicking, crying, screaming, fussing, fighting, and mad like a real *Hit Dog Hollering*. And this is not a joke; I have the BATTLE SCARS resulting from the DISOBEDIENCE that I brought on myself.

I wanted my way, and God wanted His Divine Purpose for my life to be fulfilled. God knew I lacked an understanding of my Spiritual Calling, so He was very patient with me. He nurtured, coached, and molded me into the person that was already within. He knew I would take the information and activate the Law of Reciprocity to nurture, coach, and mold others the same way He did with me.

Enough about me...let us get back to you. Have you ever had one of those days where it seems as if nothing is going right for you? When others view your issues from a different perspective, they are quick to say it is not that serious, get over it, or think positively. Well, what do you do when your issues are seriously emotionally challenging, where you cannot think at all, it feels as if you cannot get over the emotional turmoil from within, or you cannot deal with what is going on in your life? Better yet, what do you do when you have secretly lost hope or given up on life?

I am here today saying, 'There is HOPE.' How is it humanly possible to have hope, especially if we have given up? Beyond a shadow of a doubt, we have all thrown in the towel at some point in our lives. Still, there is a little resounding secret for humanity: 'As long as we have breath in our bodies, there is always HOPE!'

In the same way that the earth is designed to heal itself, we are no different. We are a part of the earth; therefore, we are entitled to this same phenomenon. However, to enforce it, *As It Pleases God*, we must know, learn, and understand how to assist ourselves in this process. If not, the earth has the Spiritual Right to reclaim its territory by any means necessary. Blasphemy, right? Wrong. *"In the sweat of your face you shall eat bread till you return to the ground, For out of it you were taken; For dust you are, And to dust you shall return."* Genesis 3:19.

When we relax, breathe, laugh, read, exercise, or experience nature, we release healing hormones to help clear our minds so we can think rationally, effectively, and fluently. These are some of the secrets to self-healing, self-motivation, self-mirroring, self-correcting, and self-esteem.

Most people want us to think that healing ourselves is difficult when it is not! You need to learn what to do, the reasons why you are doing what you do, and understand the Laws and Principles of being a good and kind person, *As It Pleases God*.

Love, Joy, Peace, Patience, Kindness, Goodness, Faithfulness, Gentleness, and Self-Control go a long way when it comes to maintaining a truly balanced lifestyle, *As It Pleases God*. Once we understand the value of 'ME' time as such, we are genuinely able to value the 'WE' time! When we properly appropriate our

'ME' time and *Overcome Distractions*, we will find that it will become an effective way to clear our heads and increase our ability to relax effectively. Try it, and you will be surprised by what a hot bath with some candles, dim lights, and soft music will do for your stressed body and mind.

Neglecting ourselves or dying a slow death from the inside out is not the ideal lifestyle. If we continue to live our lives in such a manner, or if it is not rectified in a timely manner, it will cause health problems and depression. The core of most of our health issues is usually caused by stress, selfishness, unforgiveness, anger, hatefulness, or lack of love.

When our stress is affecting us Mentally, Emotionally, Physically, or Spiritually, then it is time to do something about it. The bottom line is that you must be able to control your Level of Stress, or it will eventually control you while calling the shots without your permission. Once this happens, it will lead to the *Hit Dog Hollering*, guaranteed!

Playing Field

Regardless of whether your *Hit Dog* is hollering, panting, or yelping, if you follow my lead, you will NOT miss the mark; nevertheless, in our Predestined Blueprint, there needs to be a commitment. Yes, a commitment to regain the power over your life, a commitment from within, a commitment to your Talents, Gifts, or Calling, and most of all, a commitment to God.

What is the big deal about commitment? Suppose you can bury all the masks, defiant behaviors, or self-limiting beliefs and commit. In this case, you will find that the Holy Spirit will guide you in ways uncommon to man while leveling, neutralizing your *Playing Field*, and developing a Spiritually Positive Buffer Zone.

How do we create a Spiritual Buffer Zone? According to scripture, we must *"Set our minds on things above, not on earthly things."* Colossians 3:2. Remember, when other people are playing to win, they play with the 'By Hook or By Crook' method, which means 'By any means necessary.' So, we must be adequately equipped with the right Spiritual Tools or Weapons to keep the ball in our court while avoiding cursing our hands or Legacy in the Pursuit of Greatness. Here is what I use to neutralize my Playing Field, *As It Pleases God*:

- ☐ Respect.
- ☐ Unselfishness.
- ☐ Integrity.
- ☐ Gratefulness.
- ☐ Operating in the Will of God, *As It Pleases Him*.

When we **RESPECT** ourselves and others, it gives us the right to request respect by giving it first. In addition, it also gives the Spiritual Rights to a long life and Spiritual Respect. Our power does not reside in demanding respect; it resides in GIVING it without expecting it in return from those who pride themselves on disrespectfulness.

Would respecting a disrespectful person make us prey? We do not respect someone for their sake; we respect them for our sake and because it is the right thing to do, *As It Pleases God*. Listen, a disrespectful person, regardless of whether we respect them, ourselves, or whomever, they are going to exhibit disrespectful behavior anyway. However, if we respect ourselves, we should be able to exhibit the Fruits of the Spirit without allowing them to provoke an adverse reaction from us.

We cannot give the enemy any leverage to create strongholds or yokes in our lives when we are neutralizing our *Playing Field*.

Of course, no one is perfect, but we do have the ability to develop ourselves in a way to circumvent self-sabotage.

UNSELFISHNESS has a hidden power of LOVE most people fail to realize or take advantage of. As the scripture states, *"Do nothing out of selfish ambition or vain conceit. Rather, in humility value others above yourselves."* Philippians 2:3. Humility gives us the ability to help and serve others with no strings attached. To help someone out of the goodness of our hearts says a lot about us; plus, it opens the door for goodness to find its way back to the giver through the Law of Reciprocity.

As I take it a little further into Spiritual Unselfishness, the scriptures go a little deeper to explain how a neutralized *Playing Field* works in our favor. It says, *"Therefore, as God's chosen people, holy and dearly loved, clothe yourselves with compassion, kindness, humility, gentleness, and patience. Bear with each other and forgive one another if any of you has a grievance against someone. Forgive as the Lord forgave you. And over all these virtues put on love, which binds them all together in perfect unity."* Colossians 3:12-14.

When we exhibit **INTEGRITY** in all we do, say, and become, *As It Pleases God,* it creates a natural Spiritual Buffer that will produce a neutralized *Playing Field* by default. Really? Yes, really! *"In everything set them an example by doing what is good. In your teaching show integrity, seriousness."* Titus 2:7.

When building our Spiritual Integrity, *As It Pleases God,* it is not just about being honest with ourselves and others. There are other things required of us in the Eye of God. Here is what we must know: *"But now you must also rid yourselves of all such things as these: anger, rage, malice, slander, and filthy language from your lips. Do not lie to each other, since you have taken off your old self with its practices and have put on the new self, which is being renewed in knowledge in the image of its Creator."* Colossians 3:8-10.

GRATEFULNESS helps our mind to transition from lack to abundance. In addition, it also helps us to eradicate the addiction to approval or compliments. When we shift from man's approval to God's approval, we are better able to become used in Supernatural ways, *As It Pleases Him*. Am I pulling for straws here? Absolutely not! *"For, do I now persuade men, or God? Or do I seek to please men? If I still pleased men, I would not be a bondservant of Christ."* Galatians 1:10.

OPERATING IN THE WILL OF GOD is a great place to be. Also, in this place, we have Godly Transparency, where we lose our desire to CONTROL while becoming a CONTRIBUTOR, *As It Pleases Him*. Amazingly, this is often overlooked because we think our private moments are really private.

Moreover, we often think that if we put on a good show or secretly manipulate others, no one can tell the difference whether we are in or out of the Will of God. Well, this is our wakeup call; *"He who planted the ear, does He not hear? He who formed the eye, does He not see?"* Psalm 94:9. The moment we realize God is watching everything, we will begin to sing a different tune. Ephesians 6:6 says, *"And do this not only to please them while they are watching, but as servants of Christ, doing the will of God from your heart."*

Listen, it does not matter who we are, what we have accomplished, or our status in life. *"No one can serve two masters: Either he will hate the one and love the other, or he will be devoted to the one and despise the other. You cannot serve both God and money."* Matthew 6:24.

From my perspective, the Will of God is the SAFEST place to be; yes, a place that money cannot buy. Personally, there is nothing like having the Hand of God covering us in a Supernatural way to defy human reasoning. I am not writing about the Will of God 'just because.' I am living it, and it is for this reason I write with such passion and conviction. I do not write for me; I have been DESTINED to write according to the Will of God to bring forth the Gifts, Talents, and Calling out of those who are ready to bring forth their Hidden Genius.

In a neutralized *Playing Field*, we do not have to improvise or substitute our birthright in order to experience JOY and HAPPINESS; it is an appointed CHOICE made within the depths of our souls. Now, herein lies the problem; most of us do not know the difference. As a matter of fact, some would assume they are the same, but they are not.

Joy is experienced from within as a part of the Fruits of the Spirit or an absolute character trait once chosen. Meanwhile, happiness is experienced on the outside as it relates to someone, an experience, or a tangible item that changes based on conditions defined by us. Or, we can allow someone else to determine our happiness. If we are not a child, I would not suggest this because it will cause Mental, Physical, Emotional, and Spiritual trauma over a period of time due to unmet or superficial expectations most often set by a *Hit Dog*.

The unseen Power of God is all around and within us. If we overlook His viable sustaining Supernatural Force, we will miss out on our Birthright, as well as the benefits that come along. As a result, this puts us in an **Anything Goes** *Playing Field* to contend in areas where we may or may not be properly equipped. Here again, I would not suggest this; however, 'To each his own.' Meanwhile, before I move on, I want to say, 'God makes SENSE, and He is RELEVANT.'

The sensibility of our lives is controlled by what God has blessed us with, which are our SENSES. Most often, we do not give our senses a second thought, yet we use them constantly. Now, if we have a desire to play to win, we must fine-tune our sight, hearing, smell, taste, and touch because this is how we perceive the world in which we live.

What do our senses have to do with God? Well, let us take it to scripture, "*Our God is in the heavens; he does all that he pleases. Their idols are silver and gold, the work of human hands. They have mouths, but do not **speak**; eyes, but do not **see**. They have ears, but do not **hear**; noses, but do not **smell**. They have hands, but do not **feel**; feet, but do not walk; and they do not make a sound in their throat. Those who make them become like them; so, do all who trust in them.*" Psalm 115:3-8. So, there we have it; is this a coincidence? Absolutely not. God is all-knowing, and He is very strategic. Well, how do we convert our five senses to Spiritual Senses, *As It Pleases God*?

- ☐ **Sight.** We must protect the Gates of our Eyes from immorality, as well as its lusts. If we continue to set our eyes on waywardness, it will become a part of our consciousness by default. We must become cautious about indulging our eyes in viewing certain people, places, and things that possess the potential to beset us. According to scripture, "*The eye is the lamp of the body. So, if your eye is healthy, your whole body will be full of light, but if your eye is bad, your whole body will be full of darkness. If then the light in you is darkness, how great is the darkness!*" Matthew 6:22-23.

- ☐ **Hearing.** We must protect the Gates of our Ears from listening to negativity, chaos, and confusion. It can penetrate our state of consciousness if we are not adequately equipped to change our state of mind. On the other hand, we must not turn a deaf ear to God; we will never know how He is going to send a message, a lesson, a test, or a BLESSING. As scripture states, "*He who has ears to hear, let him hear.*" Matthew 11:15. By the same token, our Spiritual Ears must be open while channeling out the negative chatter to prevent any form of distraction, deafness, or manipulation. Why? Because our *"Faith comes from hearing, and hearing through the Word of God."* Romans 10:17.

☐ **Smell.** We must protect the Gate of our Noses because smells or aromas stimulate our minds. Therefore, we must steer clear of people, places, and things that aggravate or manipulate our sense of smell.

We all have a unique scent called pheromone, similar to that of animals, that is secreted through our glands, as well as other areas. Most of us take it for granted because we are not taught about its mind-altering effects. Our pheromones serve as an unconscious triggering agent, affecting our behavior or our level of attraction to others.

More importantly, our Spiritual Pheromones attract the people, places, and things into our lives to align our Destiny properly. So, if a scent appears to be a repellent, we must follow our instincts, especially when it comes down to our positive or negative subconscious influence. If we take it to scripture, here is what it says, *"Our lives are a Christ-like fragrance rising up to God. But this fragrance is perceived differently by those who are being saved and by those who are perishing."* 2 Corinthians 2:15.

☐ **Taste.** We must protect the Gates of our Tastes. Are we speaking of food here? I am referring to Spiritual Food...And here is what He has to say about it, *"Oh, **taste** and **see** that the Lord is good! Blessed is the man who takes refuge in him!"* Psalm 34:8. Beyond a shadow of a doubt, we know when someone or something has put a bad taste in our mouths. Plus, we also know when we are partaking in the Forbidden Fruit. We must become Spiritually Cognizant because *"Solid food is for the mature, for those who have their powers of discernment trained by constant practice to distinguish good from evil."* Hebrews 5:14.

☐ **Touch.** We must become aware of the Power of our Touch, as well as the lusts of the flesh, because it can become a double-edged sword if not used properly.

Purity and lust lie in the beholder's touch. Really? Yes, really! Let us take it to scripture to ensure we have an understanding. In our greetings, in order to avoid being RUDE, we should *"Greet one another with a holy kiss."* 2 Corinthians 13:12.

In some families or cultures, some people do not want us to touch them; therefore, we cannot violate their wishes or space. However, those who reject formal greetings will tend to have a lot more Spiritual Issues than those who greet others with a kiss, hug, nod, bow, curtsy, or handshake out of respect.

The Power of our Touch is very effective when offering love, compassion, or mercy. When we are going through the issues of life, sometimes all we need is a hug and someone to say, 'It is going to be okay.' In addition, holding someone's hand will aid in this process as well; it will also build a more solid connection in a relationship. If someone cannot hold our hands without being conscious of spreading germs, something is wrong—so, beware! Why? Germs should never take precedence over a human soul.

Now, on the flip side of the coin, if we allow the power of our touch to crossover into disrespectful lusts or perversions, then we have an even bigger problem with cursing our hands or invoking a generational curse, and sometimes it is both. The scripture says, "*Dear friends, I urge you, as foreigners and exiles, to abstain from sinful desires, which wage war against your soul.*" 1 Peter 2:11. "*So I say, let the Holy Spirit guide your lives. Then you won't be doing what your sinful nature craves.*" Galatians 5:16.

Regardless of where we are in life or what type of *Playing Field* we are on, "*It is written: Eye has not seen, nor ear heard, nor have entered into the heart of man the things which God has prepared for those who love Him.*" 1 Corinthians 2:9. Now that we have the information on leveling our playing field, let us move on to learning how to how *Iron Sharpens Iron*.

Chapter 10

Iron Sharpens Iron

When it is our time, it is our time! It is our time to reap the Fruits of our Labor, the Good of our SEEDS, or the repercussions of our folly. As life would have it, when our Season comes, there is nothing anyone or anything can do about it. But no one tells us that we must be SHARP, and dullness is not going to get it, especially in the Eye of God.

As a child of the Most High, He tells us how to conduct ourselves, the characteristics to look for, as well as the ones NOT to exhibit. He does not do this for us to pass judgment or to pretend as if we are perfect; He does it to prevent us from being fooled, manipulated, used, abused, blindsided, or led astray. James 3:13 says, *"Who is wise and understanding among you? Let them show it by their good life, by deeds done in the humility that comes from wisdom."* In my opinion, if we simply pay attention, it will save us a lot of headaches or heartaches regarding the stones that are not designed to be stepped on, turned over, or utilized, but only to serve as a lesson, and that is it!

According to the Heavenly of Heavens, our sharpness must be cultivated, nurtured, and matured, such as the Biblical concept of Seedtime and Harvest. Instead, with dullness, we begin to hoard, not giving back to the seed, becoming egotistical, judgmental, materialistic, manipulative, destructive, downright foolish, rude, selfish, or ruthless, becoming the *Hit Dog Hollering* and complaining.

Plus, if you have not noticed by now, all of your problems are created by the thoughts and beliefs about being separate, better, worse, more or less successful than others, when all you have to do is run your own race. A lot of your problems will disappear! By living your life consciously with this in mind, you are able to be fully present, Physically, Mentally, Emotionally, and Spiritually. Once you understand this, there is no competition when it comes down to your Inner Genius, even if the *Hit Dog Hollers*.

As you continue to practice living your life in Good Character, *As It Pleases God*, it brings a presence, awareness, and a peaceful stillness that allows you to go deeper into your inner self, or better yet, your true self. The true essence of who you are is wrapped in your desire to create balance from within, balance in your life, balance in your environment, and a *Spirit to Spirit* Connection.

You do not need other people, places, things, or your accomplishments to define you, to give you an identity, or to tell you who you are. You are already IT! None of that stuff is needed anymore! There is no need to chase what you already are; let it flow. I hear about the hustle all the time, but if the hustle does not come from within or is not part of your Inner Genius, Divine Blueprint, or *As It Pleases God*, then who are you really hustling?

There is nothing wrong with working for what you want or desire to become; however, you must make sure it is a part of who you are as an individual. Doing things 'just because' will not cut it, especially in the Eye of God!

Of course, *Iron Sharpens Iron*; however, you will have to work for what you want, but you must get on the right track to prevent avoidable *Do-Overs*. Unfortunately, this is the one process of life that can become very hostile and dangerous after repeated failures or defeats. Why would this become problematic? It may contain elements of disobedience, placing you in a cycle of déjà vu and fighting against yourself. How is this cycle broken? It is a little different for everyone; however, listed below are a few tips that you can graft into your specific situation, but not limited to such:

- ☐ Identify the cycle: Recognize the pattern that you are stuck in without lying to yourself.
- ☐ Determine the cause or root: Understand why you keep repeating the same behavior.
- ☐ Visualize the outcome: Imagine the positive results of breaking the cycle.
- ☐ Create new goals: Set achievable and realistic goals for yourself using a mind map, journal, or plan of action.
- ☐ Break down the cycle into smaller components: Identify the different steps that make up the cycle and tackle them one at a time.
- ☐ Develop new habits: Replace the old habits that are keeping you stuck with new, healthy ones, and add God into the equation.
- ☐ Practice mindfulness: Become more aware of your thoughts and feelings and how they influence your behavior.
- ☐ Seek support: Talk to a friend, family member, or therapist for support and guidance.

- ☐ Embrace change: Accept that change is necessary for growth, renewal, and progress.
- ☐ Take action: Take small steps towards breaking the cycle every day, Spiritually Tilling your own ground.
- ☐ Learn from your mistakes: Do not be too hard on yourself, especially if you slip up; use it as an opportunity to learn, grow, and sow back into the Kingdom.
- ☐ Stay committed: Breaking a cycle takes time and effort, but it is worth it in the end. So, do not give up on yourself.
- ☐ Prioritize self-care: Make time for activities that bring you joy and help you relax.
- ☐ Set boundaries: Learn to say no to things that are not serving you or take you out of the Will of God.
- ☐ Challenge negative self-talk: Replace negative thoughts, words, and desires with positive ones.
- ☐ Embrace imperfection: Accept that mistakes are a normal part of the learning process.
- ☐ Cultivate a growth mindset: Believe in your ability to change and grow.
- ☐ Get out of your comfort zone: Try new things and challenge yourself.
- ☐ Focus on the present moment: Avoid dwelling on the past or worrying about the future.
- ☐ Celebrate your successes: Acknowledge and celebrate your progress, no matter how small it is.

Moving forward in the Spirit of Excellence, one step at a time, makes a difference in the Eye of God. So, stop fighting with your challenges, learn from them, take the appropriate action, and share the experience with others.

You are designed to walk in your GIFTING, according to your Predestined Blueprint, without bragging or boasting about it. According to the Heavenly of Heavens, always allow the Fruits of the Spirit to speak for you. On the other hand, if you are not exhibiting the Fruits of the Spirit, then you must go back to the drawing board. Why? What you are exhibiting may not be from your Heavenly Father. When going back to the drawing board, here are a few things to do, but not limited to such:

- ☐ Practice self-compassion and self-acceptance.
- ☐ Do not insult anyone.
- ☐ Forgive and repent often.
- ☐ Apologize quickly.
- ☐ Identify and challenge negative self-talk.
- ☐ Set realistic goals and expectations for yourself.
- ☐ Celebrate your successes, no matter how small.
- ☐ Look for the good in all things.
- ☐ Cultivate a growth mindset.
- ☐ Embrace learning opportunities.
- ☐ Become more aware of your thoughts, self-talk, words, and emotions.
- ☐ Practice gratitude.
- ☐ Focus on the positive aspects of your life.
- ☐ Challenge perfectionism.
- ☐ Embrace imperfections.
- ☐ Accept that failure is part of the learning process.
- ☐ Set boundaries and learn to say no when necessary.
- ☐ Forgive yourself for past mistakes and move forward.
- ☐ Surround yourself with positive influences.
- ☐ Avoid toxic relationships.

What is the big deal about using the Fruits of the Spirit, especially when attempting to become SHARP, *As It Pleases God*? When we become rooted and grounded in the Fruits of the Spirit, self-control will naturally find its place in our lives if we exhibit Love, Joy, Peace, Patience, Kindness, Goodness, Faithfulness, and Gentleness.

If we choose not to exhibit the Fruits of the Spirit, we can still function effectively in life. However, we will have to deal with the emotional aspects of DULLNESS, which leads to bad decisions, depression, anger, hatefulness, unforgiveness, and becoming *A Hit Dog Hollering*. In so many words, we will leave ourselves open to the opposing sides of life, even if we portray ourselves as being on top of our game. Just remember, our character tells all, our attitude says even more, our behavior leaves the evidence, and our spoken words seal the deal!

How can dullness consume us as Believers? Although we have free will, disobedience is disobedience in the same way that obedience is obedience. One produces SHARPNESS and the other dullness. Here is what we must know: *"And in them the prophecy of Isaiah is fulfilled, which says: 'Hearing you will hear and shall not understand, And seeing you will see and not perceive; For the hearts of this people have grown dull. Their ears are hard of hearing, And their eyes they have closed, Lest they should see with their eyes and hear with their ears, Lest they should understand with their hearts and turn, So that I should heal them.' But blessed are your eyes for they see, and your ears for they hear; for assuredly, I say to you that many prophets and righteous men desired to see what you see, and did not see it, and to hear what you hear, and did not hear it."* Matthew 13:14-17

The bottom line is that if someone or something is putting a damper on your life, you must find a way to eliminate it. Why? *"If the ax is dull, And one does not sharpen the edge, Then he must use more strength; But wisdom brings success."* Ecclesiastes 10:10. If you cannot eliminate it, you must learn how to maneuver around it or not respond to it, especially when it is a *Hit Dog Hollering*.

Keep in mind that you are not required to respond to any and everything. But you are required to put people, places, and things into their proper perspective, *As It Pleases God*. If you do not, you cannot blame anyone besides yourself! There is no need to be rude, arrogant, abrasive, etc., because kindness will always do the trick when you set standards, boundaries, and rules when it comes down to your peace of mind. Plus, when you are honest with yourself about how you feel, why you feel this way, and who contributed to this feeling, you are then able to put the ball in your court to keep your negative feelings from getting out of control.

Your happiness depends on you! You are the one who chooses to be happy on a moment-by-moment basis. You should not let anyone or anything take this away from you! Of course, you do not live in a perfect world, and you may not be able to smile all the time, but you do not have to lose your right to be happy. Remember, happiness is a choice, but joy comes from within.

Take a moment to think about a baby or a child; they will cry for a moment, and two seconds later, they will find something to laugh about or get back to being happy. You are no different! You are still that baby or child all grown up now...and you still can laugh and be happy just because! If you are depressed right now, is it not your choice to remain this way or make a change? Absolutely! According to the root of your Faith, your change is in the here and now; own it...you got this!

Faith

When it comes down to the root of our *Faith*, we have two sides. We have the belief and the action side that bridges the gap between the tangible and the intangible elements of our *Faith*. So, let us deal with the belief side first from a Religious vs. Spiritual standpoint. If one decides to approach their roots or character from a religious standpoint, they can become limited, judgmental, divided, or deprived. On the other hand, approaching it from a Spiritual aspect, one would be able to remove the limits and love despite differences. Doing so gives us the ability to unify with others, opening ourselves up to privileged information from the Spiritual Realm.

In dealing with Religion, we must first understand it...Religion is anything we relate back to. Basically, anything can become our Religion, Faith, or Belief. A habit can become our Religion if we believe in it wholeheartedly. We can become brainwashed into certain things that can become our Religion. Actually, our past can become our Religion if we relate back to it! Unfortunately, this is how we become sifted and rooted in negativity due to the lack of understanding.

If the truth is told, sometimes Religion robs us of the ability to unite with others who are different and who are very human with emotions just like us. When whatever we relate back to divides us...It is not a good thing because we are ONE in Christ Jesus.

When we cannot love and respect our neighbors, we are out of order. Listen, we are family; we are brothers and sisters in the Kingdom of God. We are required to love each other despite what we feel or believe. Before I go any further, let me say this: No religion is 100% right or 100% wrong; they all have an element of truth; therefore, somewhere in the middle of Religion, there must be a Spiritual Covenant.

My goal is to get to the Spiritual Root, *As It Pleases God*. First and foremost, we are all Spiritual Beings having a human experience with a PURPOSE for being here. If one does not know this, they must be made aware by those who do know.

When we approach someone who lacks an understanding of who they are, we should not indulge them in cultish behaviors. Frankly, this is what causes some to turn away from God altogether.

For example, in my youth, those who were in the church were trying to brainwash me by saying, 'If I am wearing red lipstick, I am sinning.' Of course, this did not sit too well with me because my instincts and discernment told me otherwise. This church crucified me and treated me like a junkyard dog, slandering my name as if I were a nobody.

I was young, naive, and impressionable. Still, beyond a shadow of a doubt, I knew my heart was in the right place. I would not have treated anyone like they were treating me. I would not talk about someone like they talked about me, slandering my name for no reason. To add insult to injury, I would not indulge in sleeping with the Pastor, as I saw the main person who was pointing the finger.

I often wondered, 'How can a woman sleep with the Pastor and then act like a Holy Ghost-filled saint in his wife's face without a conscience?' Although out of respect, I held my tongue, but I was bewildered! Let me say this: It puzzled me and traumatized me for years until the light bulb finally went off. Most of the time, we crucify others for the same things we are secretly guilty of, presumably under a different label.

From that point on, I have believed in self-analysis, self-mirroring, and digging into my closet first while staying out of the closets of others. With this mindset, it gives me the opportunity to share information without passing judgment or pointing the finger. Instead, offering much compassion, mercy, forgiveness, and understanding, *As It Pleases God*. It is for this reason I speak mostly in the 'WE' form unless I am driving a point home, and then I will speak to 'YOU.'

When it comes down to *Iron Sharpening Iron*, I operate with a certain protocol because we are all subject to error on occasion. I do not want to curse my hand by putting down those whom God has purposed me to lift up. Most often, when it comes down to the things of the Spirit, we lack understanding in this particular area. As a result, we unknowingly curse our hands with Religious protocol and condemnation with good intentions, all in the name of our *Faith*.

God knows our hearts; however, he wants us to know the content of our hearts as well, which starts with our character. Although character traits are sometimes inherited, they can be altered by uprooting and replacing them. We cannot change where we came from, we cannot change who we are, but we can change our attitude by becoming AWARE. I always say awareness is KEY.

Once we recognize our behaviors, own them, and understand them, we can make the appropriate changes, *As It Pleases God*. Some do embark upon change without Spiritual Reasoning, but I would not suggest this. We need to know what we are doing, why we are doing so, how to do it, when to do it, where to do it, and with whom. Why? Our approach requires faith. Faith in God, faith in ourselves, and faith in applying the Fruits of the Spirit, *As It Pleases Him*.

To master our Spiritual Belief System, we must be able to apply scripture. According to the Heavenly of Heavens, this allows us to till, grow, understand, learn, know, and sow back into the Kingdom to activate the Law of Reciprocity. What is the big deal about this process? We often approach God with a giving-to-get mindset. Whereas, we are going to reverse it— we are going to GET to GIVE.

How do we make sense of the GET to GIVE mindset? We must get what we need Spiritually, and we must give it back as a SEED to build the next person as *Iron Sharpens Iron*. Does this work? Absolutely! I am living proof...this is the very SYSTEM I have used for years to gain WISDOM, Divine Wisdom, to be exact. Frankly, this is why I am bold enough to GUARANTEE what I put in writing! Not many people are able to do that!

I am not here to play around! Life has taught me the Value of Living; therefore, I am able to back up what I am saying, not out of arrogance but by CONVICTION. Out of the love I possess from within, I never want anyone to ever go through what I have gone through to get this information; therefore, I am giving the SECRETS and SHORTCUTS that will change lives from now until the end of time as *Iron Sharpens Iron*.

In this sense, when it comes down to it, our Spirituality prevails because it will cause us to hunger in a way that Religion will never feed. Let me set the record straight: I am not knocking Religion—if it works for a person, I have no qualms about that. I am promoting a *Spirit to Spirit* Relationship with our Heavenly Father, going straight to the Divine Source. Therefore, one needs an understanding so they are able to recognize deception, manipulation, negativity, bullying, or a *Hit Dog*.

According to the Heavenly of Heavens, it is not about doctrine when it comes down to the Spiritual Matters or our Predestined Blueprint; it is about WILLINGNESS and then doctrine. Blasphemy, right? Wrong. *"For it would have been better for them not to have known the way of righteousness, than having known it, to turn from the holy commandment delivered to them."* 2 Peter 2:21. Unfortunately, the doctrine is of no use if we are unwilling to use it, *As It Pleases God*.

Believe it or not, our WILL is a vital aspect of our being that is actually overlooked the most. *"If anyone is willing to do His will, he shall know concerning the doctrine, whether it is from God or whether I speak on My own authority."* John 7:17.

Most people focus on who is the smartest, who is the most intelligent, who has the most degrees, or who has the most money. But, in Spiritual Things, *As It Pleases God*, it is about who is the most WILLING! Willingness has a built-in navigational tool that guides us in a way that is SUPERNATURAL in nature. If one would open their heart with a humble willingness, saying: 'Thank you and show me the way, O Lord.' It would provide a path loaded with SEEDS leading the way toward our Divine Destiny.

It is time out for the fire and brimstone mentality; we need to usher in the Spirit of Love. Of course, we have Spiritual Laws in place to guide, protect, and keep us blessed, but nothing can replace LOVING others. Even if we feel disconnected or treated as an outcast, God has a Spiritual Bond that will bring us back into the light. Listen, no matter what we are going through, we must remember we are not alone. We are all dealing with something; therefore, we should not be casting stones. We should be mentoring or coaching others back to good grace through forgiving, letting go, and owning our truth, while exhibiting the Fruits of the Spirit.

The best way to begin the action form that puts *Faith* in motion is with Hebrews 11:1, *"Now faith is the substance of things hoped for, the evidence of things not seen."* Most think that *Faith* is some form of mystical illusion. It very well may be mystical, but it is definitely not an illusion. Actually, we all have faith, but we do not seem to recognize when we are exhibiting it.

We usually associate our faith with our wants, needs, and desires. But what about our everyday faith? The faith to wake up in the morning, the faith to sleep, the faith to eat, the faith to sit down, the faith to see, the faith to hear, the faith to touch, the faith to smell, the faith to taste, the faith to walk, the faith to do the simple things we take for granted. The most amazing part about everyday faith is that we do not realize we are using it until we become limited, handicapped, or blocked. And we have the nerve to doubt faith!

I am not knocking anyone's level of faith. At the beginning of my journey, I questioned my faith as well, especially when people were making fun of me and laughing about my walk with God. Furthermore, I did not realize my faith until it appeared to be the only thing I had left, and then I turned it into creative and executable faith.

I used scripture to hone into my gift...here is what I used, "*My tongue is the pen of a ready writer.*" Psalm 45:1. My life was in a crisis, and I was not going to engage in thinking or guessing about my next move...I had to be precise. I let loose my faith, and I have not turned back since. I have learned how to set goals, work at them, work toward them, and achieve while allowing the Creative Genius to come forth rooted in Divine Wisdom, *As It Pleased God.*

While embarking upon our root of Faith, we must understand, "*Faith comes from hearing, hearing through the Word of God.*" Romans 10:17. Therefore, when we take the Word and repeat scriptures that are applicable to our prayers or what we are going through...we actually infuse or activate it. Just as God holds us accountable for our lives, it is okay to hold God accountable for His Word. For example, we will never see a lawyer pleading his case without knowing the statutes and laws that are applicable and stating them to the Presiding Judge at the appropriate time. CASED CLOSED!

"*God has revealed it to us by the Spirit. The Spirit searches all things, even the deep things of God.*" 1 Corinthians 2:10. Once revealed, if the Spoken Words or Thoughts from the Holy Spirit are not captured immediately as a written word, they will develop wings and fly away. In my opinion, this is where a lot of us miss the mark, especially when bringing forth our Inner Genius. Why? On any level of Spirituality, documentation is KEY.

The information God shares with us cannot stop with us. If it does, from my perspective, it is a waste of information. Spiritually speaking, this is why God will stop feeding us the Secrets of the Spirit if we are not able to get what we know or His Wisdom in writing to pass it along in some way. So what, if we cannot spell, get a dictionary. What if we cannot punctuate, get a grammar book, or take a course? So what, if we cannot type, write it down in a notebook.

The bottom line is that there is no excuse not to capture great or important information. Who am I to judge, right? Absolutely. Aside from putting a demand on your Gifts, Talents, or Calling, I have been where you are right now, and I did not stop! Had I stopped, you would not be reading this book right now, and you would not be ready to step into your Destiny with such passion.

What difference would it make if we did not document? The difference is living or dying with or without documenting our journeys. What if we do not know what to say? On this note, let me ask a question: 'Who wrote the Bible?' God allowed the Holy Spirit to speak, and the person, like us, became the Spiritual Vessel to capture and document. We are no different than the writers of the Old, New, Lost, Deleted, or Stolen Testaments. We are designed to make our mark in life and for future generations with our own Testaments. So, get busy...we have a story to tell, as well as lessons, wisdom, and blessings to share.

As long as we are creating a mind map, roadmap, or documenting our progress, this ensures that we are not losing great ideas, wisdom, directions, strategies, or vital information that allows us to reflect, correct, or reject, *As It Pleases God*, creating *Stepping Stones* of Greatness.

Chapter 11
Stepping Stone

Our *Real Strength* lies in our freedom, containing viable *Stepping Stones* that we should never allow to become boulders. Unbeknown to most, as we maneuver through life, every *Hit Dog* will have a stone attached. It is our responsibility to pick up the stone to examine it for our edification, *As It Pleases God*, and learn from it to become better, stronger, and wiser to build our Cornerstones of Greatness.

I cannot begin to tell anyone the number of times I have been labeled or categorized as being weak, naive, dumb, uneducated, unpolished, unmindful, a failure, and so on. Why? I did not reveal the CARDS in my hand too early. I allowed them to carry on with their biased shenanigans, aloof antics, and negative thinking as I counteracted them with positive affirmations. Meanwhile, I kept my cool as I learned the WHY from their behavioral patterns to embrace my Divine Blueprint.

More importantly, I also used it as a *Stepping Stone*. What does *Stepping Stones* have to do with being the underdog for the *Hit Dogs Hollering*? I was in God's classroom, being about my

Father's business while they were arrogantly putting themselves on a pedestal, having to one day rely on me for Divine Wisdom, or secretly piggybacking off my ideas. What did I do when they came to me for help? To their surprise, I help them anyway. I am called to forgive, love, and help, regardless!

As a child of the Most High God, I cannot treat others the way they have treated me. If I do, then I am held to pay a higher Spiritual price, and I, personally, cannot allow my Spiritual Power to dissipate just like that! Nor do I want to become like them, creating Hit Dog Puppies...instead, I use the information and understanding I gleaned to bring forth Powerhouses, Geniuses, and Spiritual Elites, *As It Pleases God*.

Had they known the Plan of God or my Predestined Blueprint, they would have treated me better. Still, due to their Spiritual Blindness, Deafness, Muteness, Stiff Neck, and lack of Spiritual Discernment, they overlooked the CORNERSTONE to settle for the pebbles. As for the WISDOM I gleaned, it was far greater and more empowering than what I could have ever imagined.

I documented, *As It Pleased God*, with my idiosyncrasies and all. While they were laughing, making fun of my writing, and throwing me under the bus, I did not stop! And, now the *Hit Dogs Are Hollering* as God made them my footstool. Really? Yes, really!

Regardless of where we are in life or who we are, we should never degrade someone because we never know who or what a person is destined to become, similar to the story of Joseph in the Book of Genesis. Candidly, this is a story where he was favored by his father, mistreated by his brothers, stripped of his Birthright, thrown into slavery, falsely accused of rape, and then rose to the second most powerful man in Egypt without having ill will toward his offenders.

Now, let us extract some valuable Biblical Principles from Joseph. Joseph was brought up with the Spirit of Favor ingrained into his psyche by his father, Jacob. Although the overzealous favor appeared unfair to the other brothers, this is what God used to cause him to become accustomed to Spiritual Favor. In addition, this is also what God used to cause Joseph to thrive in any situation, circumstance, or event with an expectation of having a positive outcome.

But more importantly, it taught Joseph his most valuable lesson, which was to 'STOP BRAGGING.' It was this sort of arrogant behavior that caused his enslavement in the first place; besides, he had plenty of time to think about where he went wrong.

Although Joseph was enslaved, he did not allow his mind to become captured. He took his home training, etiquette, education, and skills he learned from his father's house to create a win-win situation for himself.

Nonetheless, in the midst of it all, Joseph did have human emotions like anyone else during this traumatic edifice. Do we think for a minute that Joseph did not miss the favor from his father? Do we think for a minute that Joseph did not miss his intellectual capabilities? Do we think for a minute that Joseph was not hurt due to the fact that his brothers rejected him? Do we think for a minute that Joseph did not feel the sting of some form of failure by losing his Birthright to slavery? Absolutely, who would not; however, Joseph changed his mindset to a positive faith-based trust in God, knowing God would provide regardless.

How do I know about Joseph's mindset? Because I know God. He operates in a certain way, and He rewards blessings in a certain way as well. Joseph knew Godly Principles and Protocol, as do I, and so should each one of us. In every area of temporary defeat for Joseph, God blessed him.

Why did God bless him? First and foremost, he was GRATEFUL in every situation, circumstance, or event while exuding a great attitude. Secondly, Joseph used the tools God equipped him with, such as his ability to read and write, as well as his ingenuity skills of Seedtime and Harvest, to make everything his hand touched become blessed. Thirdly, he used his Spiritual Gifts, Calling, Creativity, and Talents, as well as his prophetic abilities to interpret dreams. Fourthly, he knew about Spiritual Discipline and Spiritual Order, which are used to design or maintain any system, strategy, or concept.

We cannot go wrong giving thanks while learning to become better, not bitter. Spiritually, this is the Method of Operation for those who are Destined for Greatness. What does this mean? They overcome every obstacle with a blessing attached. If one does not know this is the way God operates, they will wallow in the 'Woe unto me Spirit.' Had Joseph been doing his own thing with a bad attitude, bragging, wallowing in negativity, being rude, and unforgiving while steering clear of his prophetic abilities, he would have become a *Hit Dog Hollering*.

How can we rewrite our lives, *As It Pleases God*, especially if we have gone astray? Our Predestined Blueprint is set; however, we can redirect our path to Spiritually Align with it, *As It Pleases Him*. Doing so forces our minds to think more without the distraction of our mouths yapping all the time like a *Hit Dog Hollering*. Is this a bit much? In my opinion, absolutely not.

For example, when we are not able to speak, by Godly design, we naturally force our Supernatural Eyes and Ears to open automatically. In my opinion, this is similar to a person who is physically blind. In contrast, their mental envisioning, hearing, audio articulation, and other senses are heightened to compensate for their loss of vision.

Does governing our tongues benefit us? Let us take it to scripture: "*If you want to enjoy life and see many happy days, keep your tongue from speaking evil and your lips from telling lies.*" 1 Peter 3:10. Better yet, "*Let no corrupt communication proceed out of your mouth, but that which is good to the use of edifying, that it may minister grace unto the hearers.*" Ephesians 4:29. The moment we are able to set a guard over our mouths, we exhibit a form of Godly self-control.

When I run into a person who cannot control what comes out of their mouth, or better yet, chooses not to control what comes out of their mouth, I know beyond a shadow of a doubt they lack self-control, period. There is a little cliché saying, *Loose lips sink ships.*' Well, today, we can UNMASK ourselves because our ship has come in, so there is no excuse for not examining our FRUITS before we allow our lips to set sail because our *Stepping Stones* depend on them.

When dealing with our *Stepping Stones*, we cannot dwell on the past. Wallowing in yesterday's mistakes is a big no-no. If there is an issue to deal with, deal with it while moving on to create a win-win or something positive without comparing. "*Do not say, 'Why were the old days better than these?' For it is not wise to ask such questions.*" Ecclesiastes 7:10.

Every *Stepping Stone* or *Hit Dog* in our lives is predicated on another. If we tiptoe around pretending as if we have nothing to work on or if we think we are absolutely perfect, we initiate the cycle of déjà vu by default. The lessons we need to learn about ourselves do not go away; they will repeat themselves until we get it.

Unfortunately, with our *Stepping Stones*, we cannot buy, manipulate, or cheat our way through this process; we must face them *As It Pleases God*. Therefore, I suggest we learn how to use the Fruits of the Spirit and mind map our way through it, while asking ourselves the right fact-finding questions to fine-tune our lessons, blessings, or testings appropriately.

When we use our *Stepping Stones* to align ourselves with the Will of God, *As It Pleases Him*, He will take care of us. There is no need to fear; all we need to do is TRUST Him, *"Look at the birds of the air, they do not sow, nor reap nor gather into barns, and yet your heavenly Father feeds them. Are you not worth much more than they?"* Matthew 6:26. Of course, we are...we are all important in the Sight of God, and He needs us to fulfill our Mission in Life. Trust that it takes the same amount of energy to pursue our Purpose as it would to avoid it; therefore, it behooves us to stop wasting time on people, places, and things contradicting what we are called to do. *"Therefore, everyone who hears these Words of Mine and puts them into practice is like a wise man who built his house on the rock."* Matthew 7:24.

From my perspective, every emotion, thought, feeling, obstacle, stronghold, affliction, sickness, healing, or whatever has a *Stepping Stone* associated. Thus, it is our responsibility to seek the truth from scripture, pray, repent, forgive, fast, and meditate in order to align ourselves with our Predestined Blueprint, *As It Pleases God*.

Can we get to our Divine Destiny any other way? Yes, with a lot of trial and error, a lot of déjà vu, a lot of failures, a lot of setbacks, and the list goes on. In my opinion, it is always best to learn from a wise man than a fool! But more importantly, let us take it to scripture, *"Be very careful, then, how you live—not as unwise but as wise, making the most of every opportunity, because the days are evil."* Ephesians 5:15-16. *"To the person who pleases Him, God gives wisdom, knowledge, and happiness, but to the sinner he gives the task of gathering and storing up wealth to hand it over to the one who pleases God. This too is meaningless, a chasing after the wind."* Ecclesiastes 2:26.

As we move on, here is one scripture I want to drive home: *"The wisdom that comes from heaven is first of all pure; then peace-loving, considerate, submissive, full of mercy and good fruit, impartial and sincere."* James 3:17. For me, if someone proclaims to have the Wisdom of God, I look for their PEOPLE SKILLS. I watch to see if they are exhibiting the characteristics of this scripture. Suppose I see uncanny chaos, hatefulness, selfishness, disobedience, unforgiveness, unfairness, untrustworthiness, or the absence of the Fruits of the Spirit. In this case, I know it is not of God, and my Spiritual Antennas go up in full effect, not out of judgment, but to protect my Spiritual Anointing.

The *Stepping Stones* leading to our Predestined Blueprint, *As It Pleases God*, requires us to lead ourselves and others from the bottom first, with clean hands and a pure heart. If we are able to lead from where we are in the pursuit of what God has for us, we will not miss the MARK. What is the MARK? It is different for everyone; therefore, we must develop a *Spirit to Spirit* Relationship with our Heavenly Father for updates and details.

As a matter of fact, once we are able to influence others from the BOTTOM, God will trust us enough to influence from the TOP. Now, here is where a lot of us get derailed; we are trying to step into Purpose from the top like a Big Dog, Spiritual Giant, or a bullying *Hit Dog Hollering*! In the Realm of the Spirit, it just does not work like this; we have to put in the work, *As It Pleases Him*.

There are levels and notches when it comes to Spirituality, dealing with our Divine Destiny. Unfortunately, this is not a free-for-all, and this is why a lot of people give up on their dreams to retreat to the familiar. It requires us to suit up Spiritually, *As It Pleases God*. Meanwhile, most people do not want to alter their lifestyle to assume their rightful place in the

Kingdom. Nor do they have a desire to put in double duty to bring forth the Genius from Within.

Listen, as I keep it real, we cannot step into Divine Greatness without being fully equipped, *As It Pleases God*; it is dangerous! Why? It is Spiritually Guarded to prevent illegal entry or the misuse of Kingdom Edifices. Frankly, this is why our *Stepping Stones* come in to adequately train us to deal with success or how to deal with the issues of life from God's Divine Perspective.

Of course, *Iron Sharpens Iron*, but our *Stepping Stones* are just as SHARP, circumcising us from worldly to Spiritual as we develop a *Spirit to Spirit* Connection, *As It Pleases God*.

Thus, you will have to work for what you want, Spiritually Tilling your own ground and examining yourself, *As It Pleases God*. What is the purpose of doing so? When it is all said and done, all we need to do is ask for revelation, Divine Revelation, to be exact.

Do we think for a minute that God will deny us ordinary revelation or Divine Revelation of ourselves, especially when dealing with our *Stepping Stones*? No, He will not because we all need Spiritual Examination from time to time, similar to when Jesus advised the Twelve Disciples that someone was going to betray Him. "*And they were exceedingly sorrowful, and began every one of them to say unto him, Lord, is it I?*" Matthew 26:22.

Nevertheless, we must become fully in tune when He sends the answer because we never know how He is going to send it or from whom. It may come as a lesson, a spoken word, a sign, a person, an animal, a quote, a question, a statement, and the list goes on. Here is Jesus' response to the Twelve, "*He who dipped his hand with Me in the dish will betray Me.*" Matthew 26:23.

Point in fact, God may send our answer in a riddle, an experience, or whatever; therefore, our Spiritual Antennas must be on point and alert to ensure we do not miss out or miss it. Conversely, as a part of our Spiritual Protocol, we must ASK the question, SEEK the answer, and we will FIND. Okay, now let us take it to scripture: *"Ask, and it shall be given you; seek, and ye shall find; knock, and it shall be opened unto you."* Matthew 7:7.

Most often, we do not ask because we are afraid of the answer, we do not want to hear the answer, we are oblivious to the answer, or we are on the run from the answer. But God is not worried or amazed at all; He knows it is only a matter of time before our Spiritual Consciousness will seek out the TRUTH. Besides, the most remarkable aspect of this process is that when we are ready, He is too.

Chapter 12
Multiplying Factors

Can we multiply when a *Hit Dog Is Hollering*? Absolutely. When we place God first, *As It Pleases Him*, He can restructure everything based on this one Spiritual Decree: *'Be Fruitful and Multiply.'* He does not say, *'Be selfish and Spoil!'* Throughout my life, I have seen people who are cursed while being very rich. I have seen those who are very blessed while being stricken by poverty. I have seen others who are both cursed and stricken by poverty while celebrating their wretchedness without any form of recourse. Then I have also seen those who are wealthy, Mentally, Physically, Emotionally, Spiritually, and Financially, living their best lives, *As It Pleases God*.

According to the Heavenly of Heavens, *A Hit Dog Will Holler* when Spiritual Principles and Wealth are NOT obtained, *As It Pleases God*. Why? The void from within will cause us to lash out, attempting to soothe the psyche, not realizing there is no SALVE outside of God Almighty. There is only a need for SALVATION. What makes this so important? Spiritual Wealth is the desired place of ultimate PURPOSE, but we must have Spiritual Principles in place to capitalize, *As It Pleases Him*, making it possible to achieve by all but used only by a few. Really? Yes, really!

Without pursuing Divine Purpose or unveiling our Predestined Blueprint, *As It Pleases God*, we will become lost like a drifting ship at sea. We can deny this all we like or allow our *Hit Dogs To Holler*, but here is what we must know: "*For we are God's fellow workers; you are God's field, God's building. According to the grace of God which was given to me, like a wise master builder I laid a foundation, and another is building on it. But each man must be careful how he builds on it. For no man can lay a foundation other than the one which is laid, which is Jesus Christ.*" 1 Corinthians 3:9-11.

The Divine Presence of God is more active than we could care to imagine. As the scripture states, "*God is our refuge and strength; a very present help in trouble.*" Psalm 46:1. All we need to do is make the request known or call out to God, right? Absolutely. The scripture states, "*Trust in Him at all times, O people; pour out your hearts before Him.*" Psalm 62:8.

How often do we forget to reach out to God, trying to handle things on our own? Realistically, it happens all too often that we find ourselves having to backtrack to have God clean up our messes. Then, we have the nerve to play pretend or the victim as if we have done nothing wrong while throwing rocks, hiding our hands, and deflecting like *A Hit Dog Hollering*.

Oh, do not pretend...we have all had our share of messes. The moment we overlook our messes without correcting or surrendering them, we make an even bigger mess. Regrettably, so much so that we have dug ourselves into a little ditch where we are scraping the bottom and forced to give it to God.

Clearly, I do not wish a mess upon anyone; I am simply painting a picture of what could happen if we play by our own rules and not God's. However, I do suggest using the Power of

God's Hand, as well as the power of His Finger, when dealing with the issues of life. Why? Simply put, according to scripture, *"I have been young, and now am old; yet have I not seen the righteous forsaken, nor his seed begging bread."* Psalm 37:25.

Why would someone intentionally create their bed of suffering? Most often, we do not wish suffering on ourselves. We only lack the understanding of the repercussions of what we are doing, saying, and becoming because we are getting what we want. Then again, this could very well be a selfish or selfless act; who knows, besides the person from within, right?

We rationalize and justify all the time; however, when it comes down to the root of our character, we must choose! We have to draw a line in the sand on whether we are on the positive or negative, right or wrong, or good or evil side. Side of what exactly? We must decide if we will remain on the side of the Kingdom of God or continue in worldliness.

In the Eye of God, when dealing with *Multiplying Factors*, straddling the fence cannot be an option. Why can we not straddle, especially when having free will? We are under a Spiritual Multiplying Covenant. Here is what we must know: *"For when God made a promise to Abraham, because He could swear by no one greater, He swore by Himself, saying, 'Surely blessing I will bless you, and multiplying I will multiply you.'"* Hebrews 6:13-14.

More importantly, we must remain on the obedient side of this Spiritual Covenant, or it can work against us. How is this possible, especially when there is no Contingency Clause? Oh, but there is one. *"When Abram was ninety-nine years old, the LORD appeared to Abram and said to him, 'I am Almighty God; walk before Me and be blameless. And I will make My covenant between Me and you, and will multiply you exceedingly.' Then Abram fell on his face, and God talked with him, saying: 'As for Me, behold, My covenant is with you, and you shall be a father of many nations."* Genesis 17:1-4.

How do we replace ungodly with Godly? We must reverse our character traits from negative to positive, *As It Pleases Him*. Listed below are a few examples, but not limited to such:

- ☐ Replace Hate with Love.
- ☐ Replace Unforgiveness with Forgiveness.
- ☐ Replace Callousness with Compassion.
- ☐ Replace Hatefulness with Kindness.
- ☐ Replace Selfishness with Selflessness.
- ☐ Replace Arrogance with Humility.
- ☐ Replace Doubtfulness with Courage.
- ☐ Replace Fear with Faith.
- ☐ Replace Hopelessness with Hope.
- ☐ Replace Indifference with Commitment.
- ☐ Replace Impatience with Patience.
- ☐ Replace Abrasiveness with Gentleness.
- ☐ Replace Self-Indulgence with Self-Control.
- ☐ Replace Chaos with Peace.
- ☐ Replace Anxiousness with Patience.
- ☐ Replace Unjustness with Fairness.
- ☐ Replace Lying with Truthfulness.
- ☐ Replace Dishonesty with Honesty.
- ☐ Replace Narrow-mindedness with Open-mindedness.
- ☐ Replace Unreliability with Dependability.
- ☐ Replace Irresponsibility with Responsibility.
- ☐ Replace Waywardness with Integrity.
- ☐ Replace Ungratefulness with Gratitude.
- ☐ Replace Folly with Wisdom.
- ☐ Replace Unreliability with Trustworthiness.
- ☐ Replace Anger with Peacefulness.
- ☐ Replace Laziness with Diligence.
- ☐ Replace Rudeness with Respectfulness.
- ☐ Replace Failure with Success.

- ☐ Replace Misunderstanding with Understanding.
- ☐ Replace Intolerance with Tolerance.
- ☐ Replace Unteachability with Teachability.

Does it really matter if we replace them or not? In the Eye of God, it matters. As we meander through life, we often do not realize our hands have significant power, nor do we take into account the power of our fingers as well. Although we do not think about the use of our hands or fingers often, we simply use them by default. As a matter of fact, we do not realize that life and death are in the power of our hands, similar to the scripture saying, *"Death and life are in the power of the tongue, and those who love it will eat its fruit."* Proverbs 12:21. Why must we know this? The *Hand to Finger Approach* is tied to our *Multiplying Factors*.

Hand To Finger Approach

Through the *Hand to Finger Approach*, my goal is to bring about conscious awareness, as well as the revelation regarding the power we possess with what comes out of our mouths and the power we have in our hands. This hidden Secret of the Ancient of Days helps us to maximize the Power of God's Hand and Finger simultaneously.

What is the difference between God's Hand and Finger? The Power of God's Hand is used for general or non-specific issues for Spiritual Covering, Guidance, or Empowerment. Meanwhile, the Power of God's Finger points toward something specific for His Divine Touch, Restoration, or Regrafting. How do we make this make sense? For example, but not limited to such:

- ☐ **General Issue**: Invoking God's Hand over our minds.

- ☐ **Specific Issue:** Invoking God's Finger over the thoughts of defeat.

- ☐ **General Issue:** Invoking God's Hand over our health.
- ☐ **Specific Issue:** Invoking God's Finger for overeating cupcakes at midnight.

- ☐ **General Issue:** Invoking God's Hand over our anger.
- ☐ **Specific Issue:** Invoking God's Finger over the inability to deal with rejection.

This is similar to having a Doctor in a General Practice, and then we have Doctors who specialize in something specific. Besides, when dealing with God, it is best to get to the root of the issue in order to regraft or uproot, as opposed to skimming over the surface to patch up the problem without healing, restoring, or uprooting. Furthermore, knowing when to petition for God's Hand or Finger will make a big difference in finetuning the Language of our Heavenly Father, as well as maximizing our ability to put the pieces of our lives back into the appropriate perspective, *As It Pleases Him.*

How do we know if the Finger of God is in our lives? He says, *"I with the Finger of God cast out devils, no doubt the kingdom of God has come upon you."* Luke 11:20. When we own our truth regarding who God has created us to be, allow the Holy Spirit to become ONE with ours, operate in the Spirit of Obedience, and apply the Fruits of the Spirit in our lives, we will have the POWER to take up our rod as Moses did, using what we have in our hands.

Of course, this is not about a magic trick or pretending—the power we are looking for in others lies within the depths of our souls as well. If it is healing that we need, we have the power. If we need encouragement, we have the power to encourage ourselves. If we need to cast down a wayward Spirit, we have the power to command our release. Whatever we need, we have the power! We simply need to know it and own it. How should we model our *Hand to Finger* Prayer request? Here is how I would preface this prayer:

If I, by the Finger of God with the Holy Seal of Grace, hereby command with the Unction of the Holy Spirit to ___*(state the specific request or action)*___, in the Name of Jesus. By the Authority Vested in me, I declare and decree the Hand of God over ___*(state the general request or action)*___.

What if we opt not to use our power? If we do not realize or utilize our power, *As It Pleases God*, we will begin to play church. Then again, we may become a wolf in sheep's clothing or ostracize others without exhibiting compassion or mercy for what we are secretly guilty of. Unfortunately, in the Eye of God, this becomes problematic, causing us to turn on ourselves or become the *Hit Dog Hollering*.

Listen, even if one does not understand anything from this book, here is what I need everyone to know: God is MOVED by certain behaviors, characteristics, and qualities, positively or negatively. For the record, our Supernatural Power, Favor, and Grace reside in exhibiting them positively, with forgiveness, compassion, and mercy as our reason to do so. What does this mean? We have regular power, and then we have Supernatural Power. One requires God, using Spiritual Principles, and the other one does not, but is still available to all.

The moment I discovered how to negotiate with God, I have not taken this for granted since. I have some say that we cannot negotiate with God, but I beg to differ. In life, one thing I have found is that 'Everything is Negotiable!'

In the *Spirit to Spirit* Relationship that I have with God, I do not go to Him half-stepping or begging. I go with scriptures, line upon line and precept upon precept. Why? I do not go to Him, relying on grace to save me or approach Him empty-handed. I go with Spiritual Principles, Laws, Concepts, and Precepts while using my Fruits of the Spirit as Divine Leverage. More importantly, I use grace as my backup plan, just in case I miss something. Does it work? Absolutely. Not only that, but it also gives me the opportunity to create a win-win situation out of everything, or find the opportunity in the problem to document like I am doing now.

Divine Reformation

Now, the question is, 'How long does it take to develop into a Spiritual Elite, *As It Pleases God*?' We are not zapped into Elite Status or become a superhero overnight. Unbeknown to most, there is a Spiritual Training Process or Spiritual Cleansing Process that is required. In the Eye of God, the Regrafting of our Character takes time; however, this should not detour us from the process.

In my opinion, we can start now to get it over with. Or, we can continue on the same path, playing pretend, having to come back to this same point at some other time. Now, after saying this, let me formally answer the question. Leviticus 19:24 says, "*In the fourth year all its fruit will be holy, an offering of praise to the LORD.*" This scripture refers to the planting of any fresh fruit tree...on this Spiritual Journey, you are the FRESH FRUIT. Spiritually, this is what you will become known by, and you will need to learn how to exhibit the Fruits of the Spirit in order to develop into a REAL Spiritual Elite, *As It Pleases God*.

According to scripture, for three years, your Fruit is forbidden and should not be consumed because you are still growing, understanding, being purified, being taught, being molded, and being tested. When you violate this, people get hurt, especially in the CHURCH.

For example, someone gets saved on Sunday and preaches to the masses on Monday to deliver them without taking time out to get themselves fully delivered, *As It Pleases God!* Most often, this is how negative Spiritual Transfers get us wrapped in bondage. When this happens, there are still Spiritual Strongholds that must come out...lest one will begin to do the right things for the wrong reasons. Unfortunately, this is why there is more hurt, debauchery, deception, mind-control, judgment, and betrayal in the CHURCH than in the secular world.

Now, getting back on track, in the 4th year, your Spiritual Eliteness becomes holy and an offering to God. Once you are offered up, *As It Pleases God* in this manner, you become anointed and HIGHLY favored, giving you the power to speak volumes to God through your INNER MAN without you having to open your physical mouth.

In the 5th year, your Spiritual Eliteness is appropriate for consumption by those who are placed in your path. Trust that those who are placed in your path after the 5th year need what you have to offer. Most would think five years is too long when they need it now. And I will say it again: You already have what you need; you were born with it; however, it is tainted with worldliness. Therefore, the Holy Spirit must do a SPIRITUAL CLEANSING on you, washing you with the Blood of Jesus, even if you feel as if you do not need it.

In order to bear the Fruits of the Spirit as you should, Hebrews 13:15 says, *"Through Jesus, therefore, let us continually offer to God a sacrifice of praise—the fruit of lips that confess his name."* Paul is saying that you need to offer a 'sacrifice' of praise or an 'offering' to God with your prayers, your resources, your time, your energy, and the fruits of your lips. How? It is done verbally through prayer, praise, worship, words, conversations, and so on in a *Spirit to Spirit* Relationship, confessing His name or exhibiting the Fruits of the Spirit, *As It Pleases Him.*

Praising God through good deeds, good faith, good beliefs, good adornment, or good respect are just as good as confessing His name. The only difference is that you are using His Fruits of the Spirit to deliver the same praise, message, or partnership that is contrary to what is being taught by others. I am not saying that you do not need to pray, fast, and read your Bible, because you do! I do not want you to stop there; there is more to God than the 'Sermon on the Mount.' There is 'Doing on the Mount.' There is 'Becoming on the Mount.' There is 'Being on the Mount.' And there is 'Fruit on the Mount' as well, which must be shared with others. Downplaying or ignoring the use of the Fruits of the Spirit creates dysfunction among those who pretend to be more than what they are.

God is challenging you to take the time to develop the Voice of Volumes through the Fruits of the Spirit, as opposed to the standard run-of-the-mill worship. Dare to be different, dare to expose your Inner Greatness, dare to sing a new song that is uniquely yours via the Holy Spirit, to glorify and exalt your Heavenly Father.

The Divine Plan

Someplace in the midst of Divine Planning, long before your parents ever thought about you, you were on God's mind! So much so, He formulated a unique BLUEPRINT with a perfect PLAN just for you that is unlike any other.

In His Divine Plan, you were preordained to become who you are with no shame attached to it. But there is one obstacle standing between you and God's perfect will for your life. What is it? You must CHOOSE to walk according to the Divine Plan He has ordained for you.

God seeks ways to approach each of us in order to introduce our Predestined Blueprint for our lives, but we must allow Him in. He encourages us to accept Christ as our Lord and Savior. If we accept, we take our first step into understanding our MISSION. But if we resist Him, we will become lost or caught up in the issues of life.

The Holy Spirit listens intently to each detail of your life as it was planned at birth, and He waits for His cue to reveal your uniqueness, your ministry, or your success to you. In fact, the Holy Spirit is the One who has been put in charge of overseeing God's Divine Plan for you. Make no mistake about it: He searches your heart constantly to nudge and guide you; however, He will not override your free will or natural laws when you are not under Divine Subjection.

The natural laws governing the conditions around you will control you if you do not realize who you are or what you possess from within. However, natural laws are secondary to the Spiritual Laws of the Land. God may not enforce Spiritual Laws in your favor or break natural laws for you if you are clueless or careless about Him or His Divine Plan for your life. Spiritually, this is why the Holy Spirit continually searches your heart to convict you or get rid of everything contrary to the Will of God, if you allow Him to do so.

Contrary to what you may believe or what you may have been taught, it is impossible to discover your Divine Blueprint by simply reading the Bible alone. Now, the Word of God (The Bible) will indeed teach about His Spiritual Laws, Concepts, Precepts, and Strategies. It will guide you...it will encourage you...it will teach you...You may learn all about salvation, healing, prosperity, righteousness, Heaven and Hell, and

Biblical stories. Actually, it will do a lot of things for you, except CHOOSE for you, reveal your calling to you, or grant you WISDOM! Spiritually, this is the job of the Holy Spirit.

The moment you wholeheartedly choose your Predestined Blueprint, you open the door to Divine Wisdom, which will begin to guide you instinctively. Now, let me say this: Most people think they are wise when they are just really knowledgeable. Divine Wisdom requires a direct connection to the Holy Spirit, period! There is no way around it.

Once you awaken your Spirit and connect with the Holy Spirit, it opens a reservoir of wisdom, guidance, counsel, and power that takes you to another level of Spirituality that everyone will not experience. And, yes, we may know how to pray and claim our inheritance, we may know how to fast and pray for healing or restoration, we may know how to pray for provision, and we may know how to do a lot of things Spiritually. Nevertheless, when it comes down to our Predestined Blueprint, it releases a tremendous amount of POWER from within that will leave demons trembling in their boots. The only thing about this amount of POWER is that we need to realize we have it, lay claim to it, unveil our calling, and share it while exhibiting the Fruits of the Spirit!

Prayer Closet

The moment you decide to embark upon your Predestined Blueprint, get yourself a real PRAYER CLOSET or a DESIGNATED PLACE to spend some quality time with the Lord in prayer, *Spirit to Spirit*. Really? Yes, really! Matthew 6:6 says, *"But thou, when thou prayest, enter into thy closet, and when thou hast shut thy door, pray to thy Father which is in secret; and thy Father which seeth in secret shall reward thee openly."* In the Eye of God, this is indeed the moment you will enter into your Spiritual Classroom with the Holy Spirit as your INSTRUCTOR.

Your time alone in your *Prayer Closet* is where the unveiling of your Divine Blueprint will take place. Of course, you will need to incorporate some form of fasting, but whatever you do, this is between you and God. If you faithfully continue to get to know God in this manner, one year from now, you will not be the same, guaranteed! When you pursue God in this manner, your Spiritual Growth and wisdom will trump anything you would have ever imagined.

The best time of the day for getting closer to your Powerhouse with God is first thing in the morning. Spiritual warfare and covenants take place at night or in the wee hours of the morning in our dreams, as well as in our moments of darkness. At daybreak, it is always best to get rid of or filter out, rebuke, or cancel anything that is not conducive to the will of God. I have found this to be a profound Spiritual way of combating every form of negativity, Spiritual Attacks, or ill wishes. By doing so, it reverses the negative into good, positive, and fruitful things, actions, or thoughts before you begin your day. How often have you heard about this? Not much, right?

Let me say this: It is your responsibility to take hold of or bless your day by going into your *Prayer Closet* every morning except for Saturdays, unless it is an emergency, to release, rejuvenate, and restore your Powerhouse to ensure you remain effective, influential, and powerful.

Praising the Lord in the morning will become second nature to you once you realize how much POWER you have over your day. Praise and worship are indeed things God wants you to do, and He wants you to do them as naturally as breathing. In my opinion, when you include the Book of Psalms as a part of your daily regimen and the Book of Proverbs as your character-forming guide, you are well on your way to becoming the Powerhouse of your days.

In conclusion, Psalm 37:5 says, *"Commit your way to the Lord, Trust also in Him, And He shall bring it to pass."* And, *"Delight yourself in the Lord, and he will give you the desires of your heart."* Psalm 37:4. Many Blessings...as you Grow Great!

Dr. Y. Bur

www.DrYBur.com

www.ingramcontent.com/pod-product-compliance
Lightning Source LLC
Chambersburg PA
CBHW071445160426
43195CB00013B/2035